Philosophy and Politics

EDITED BY

G. M. K. Hunt

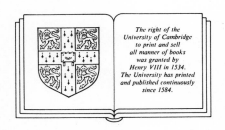

The right of the
University of Cambridge
to print and sell
all manner of books
was granted by
Henry VIII in 1534.
The University has printed
and published continuously
since 1584.

CAMBRIDGE UNIVERSITY PRESS

CAMBRIDGE
NEW YORK PORT CHESTER MELBOURNE SYDNEY

Published by the Press Syndicate of the University of Cambridge
The Pitt Building, Trumpington Street, Cambridge, CB2 1RP
40 West 20th Street, New York, NY 10011, USA
10 Stamford Road, Oakleigh, Melbourne 3166, Australia

British Library Cataloguing in Publication Data

Philosophy and politics: supplement to Philosophy 1989
(Royal Institute of Philosophy lecture series; 26).
1. Politics. Theories
I. Hunt, G. M. K. II. Series
320.01
ISBN 0 521 39597 6

Library of Congress Cataloguing in Publication Data

Philosophy and politics/edited by G. M. K. Hunt
p. cm. – (Royal Institute of Philosophy lectures: 26)
'Supplement to Philosophy 1989'
Includes index.
ISBN 0 521 39597 6
1. Political science – Philosophy. I. Hunt, G. M. K.
II. Philosophy (London, England). 1989 (Supplement)
III. Series:
Royal Institute of Philosophy lectures: v. 26.
B65.P548 1990   90-38806
320'.01—dc20   CIP

Origination by Precise Printing Company Ltd, Reigate, Surrey
Printed in Great Britain by the University Press, Cambridge

Egalitarianism—
Miller quoting Tocqville
unreliable

Contents

2 Contrast to Hayek assertion, egalitarianism Minogue
p 103 — the depraved, independent

List of Contributors

Norman Barry MA
  Professor of Politics, University of Buckingham

Peter Binns BA, BPhil
  Lecturer in Philosophy, University of Warwick

Don Locke MA, BPhil
  Emeritus Professor of Philosophy, University of Warwick

Susan Mendus BA, BPhil
  Lecturer in Philosophy, University of York

David Miller MA, DPhil
  Nuffield College, Oxford

Kenneth Minogue BA, BSc
  Professor of Government, London School of Economics

A. Phillips Griffiths BA, BPhil
  Professor of Philosophy, University of Warwick
  Director of the Royal Institute of Philosophy

J. Enoch Powell PC MBE
  Member of Parliament 1950–1987
  Minister of Health 1960–1963

Robert Skidelsky MA, DPhil, FRHistS, FRSL
Professor of International Studies, University of Warwick

G. W. Smith BA, PhD
  Lecturer in Politics and International Relations, University of Lancaster

Preface

This varied collection explores a recurrent theme connecting philosophy and politics: the relation between the nature of man and the structure of society. This is by no means the only intersection of interests between politics and philosophy—the contemporary collaboration on methodological issues has led political science to rival political theory—but it is above all the common concern of philosophy and politics with the nature of man as an essentially social being. This current collection approaches this absorbing problem by concentrating on the topical issue of the market economy, viewed as an attempt to resolve the clash between individual autonomy and collective action.

The thesis is that democracy, the ideal of summing individual desires into an aggregate intention, is best realized through the market. An individual's votes (or pounds as they are often called) are allotted in proportion to rendition of service to others. The aggregation of the votes follows from their being used to buy the services of many others. The power of the individual is in proportion to his serving others. The power of society is no more than the sum of the independent votes of its members, and democratic equality is guaranteed by common currency. Society is just the exchange of services. As the essays show, this market thesis is sometimes thought necessary for a democratic society, sometimes wholly sufficient.

Would that it were so simple. The antithesis defended in a number of the essays shows that the assumptions about the nature of the individual which lie behind the market analysis are more complex than might be supposed. The individual may not be as autonomous as is required by market theory. The view that an individual's personality is a social construction is at variance with the foundational role personal decisions play in market theory. Further, an individual's religious, ethical and social rules may conflict with particular desires and wishes as they are felt at each market transaction. For example, an egalitarian ethic may override a sensible particular decision about the value of a service. Personal interactions are thus mediated through social and ideological constructions.

The substance of this wide ranging debate centres on whether, and how, these difficulties can be resolved. It involves thinkers whose views differ greatly. Enoch Powell begins with an historical and personal

Preface

recollection (with a response by Robert Skidelsky), and the essays that follow allow political theorists and philosophers to take issue on each of the topics of Markets and Morals, Liberal Man, Equality and Libertarianism.

The volume is aimed at the general reader who wishes to understand the deeper issues in the current debate over the proper role of the market in a liberal democratic society, but is also very suitable for students and teachers of senior classes, both for examination courses and supplementary studies. The essays were originally delivered to an audience of sixth form and Further Education teachers. The book adds a summary article by A. Phillips Griffiths, Director of the Royal Institute of Philosophy.

G. M. K. Hunt
University of Warwick

Theory and Practice

J. ENOCH POWELL

I intend, here, in reflecting on my life to see if, by taking what appear to me in retrospect to be three critical points of vantage from which to describe my situation, my intentions and the thought, if any, which lay behind them, I can be of service.

I start in February, 1946. I am still wearing the King's uniform, which I have worn for the previous six and a half years, and I have just returned to England after an absence of nearly five years, of which the last two and half have been spent in India. Having reconciled myself more or less reluctantly to the uncovenanted bonus of a probable normal length of life, I have already asked myself what I intend to do with it; and that other self, which stands there on the doorstep when you open the door, like an unwanted caller, has given me the answer: 'You are going into politics.' But why? A negative reason first: I never meant to go back to a university, for I felt that I would be smothered there and eaten alive. But why politics? I had not only no sympathy, but deep hostility during the 1930s towards the Conservative governments of the United Kingdom, which I regarded as having been purblind to the situation in which the United Kingdom found itself and having pushed to the extremity of danger the safety and survival of . . ., and I would undoubtedly have followed the preposition 'of' at that time with the words 'the British Empire', for, in 1939 it was in fact the British Commonwealth and Empire, which, in a somewhat ragged fashion, did at last and belatedly go to war, and I had participated in my own way in the success with which that structure, if it *was* a structure, had defended itself and, if it survived, had survived. As I mentioned, the last two and a half years had been in India, the centre in many ways, emotionally, organizationally, and strategically, of that conglomeration, and it seemed to me, that the way things were going there pointed to dissolution. There is a saying (I hope I attribute it correctly to Burke, and I hope I locate it correctly in the trial of Warren Hastings) to the effect that 'the keys of India are not in Calcutta, they are not in Delhi, they are on the dispatch box in the House of Commons'. I certainly believed, wrongly, that the necessary willpower and the necessary decisions were still located there in 1946, and I wished, in this uncovenanted extension of my life, to take a hand in the governance of India. The route was to be the route to that key—through Parliament and via the despatch box.

1

So, I had answered my own question with the reply 'You are going into politics', and within 24 hours of landing at Brize Norton—and on landing at Brize Norton I remember weeping when I saw green fields—I looked up 'C' in the telephone directory, 'C' for 'Conservative', for 'Conservative Central Office'. Now, why, having already indicated my total antipathy to the Conservative Party and successive Conservative governments as I had known them before 1939? Because I supposed that, if there was to be a vehicle and a framework for what I imagined I would be doing, it had to be the Conservative Party. I was born a Tory. Define: a Tory is a person who regards authority as immanent in institutions. I had always been, as far back as I could remember in my existence, a respecter of institutions, a respecter of monarchy, a respecter of the deposit of history, a respecter of everything in which authority was capable of being embodied, and that must surely be what the Conservative Party was about, the Conservative Party as the party of the maintenance of acknowledged prescriptive authority. (I would not at that stage have yet been using the term 'prescriptive' as readily as I was to train myself afterwards to use it.) There was something else; it would be a party which did not believe in always starting afresh over and over again, it would be a non-innovatory party, a party which chimed in, therefore, with my own prejudices and nature. Anyhow, 'C' it was in the London telephone directory. Within a fortnight I was already on the speakers panel; I was already (it was much easier in those days) on the candidates list; and I was already employed in the Conservative Parliamentary Secretariat, which did its best to supply information to the sorely depleted Opposition Front Bench of 1946.

Pitchforked into an array of internal politics, pitchforked into Parliamentary politics as they were in the 1940s, I set about the business of getting myself a seat, which I did not achieve until the end of 1948 after something like twenty rebuffs from other constituencies before Wolverhampton South-West. They were years in which I read voraciously in political history, in constitutional history. (Some of the results found their way into a book on the House of Lords in the Middle Ages which was published in 1968.) And I began to practise my trade.

Before long, I was overtaken by the events of 1947 and the acceptance by the Conservative Party in Parliament of the inevitability of the separation of India from the rest of the British Empire and Commonwealth. So, the basis on which my decision had been taken no longer existed. I was bereft of the ground on which I thought I was treading when I walked into Conservative Central Office in March 1946. But I was not entirely, by then, unprepared for handling this shock, a shock so severe that I remember spending the whole of one night walking the streets of London trying to come to terms with it. Being an aspirant for the House of Commons, I had begun to familiarize myself with the nature of that extraordinary assembly and its central position in the politics and governance of my own country, a subject on which, before that, I had been woefully ignorant and unreflective; and I was feeling my way towards understanding the axiom of government subject to parliamentary representation, namely that such government cannot logically extend over populations which cannot be there represented. It was the old proposition of the American Colonies, (by which I was later to understand that my own country had been haunted for the best part of two centuries,) to which I was already addressing myself and which I had begun to grasp sufficiently to perceive dimly the contradictory nature, as the earliest of the British in India had understood it, of British rule in India, the responsibility of the representative of Wolverhampton South-West for the governance of a population which could never be represented in the Parliament of the United Kingdom.

Something else was also happening during these years in which the gound fell away from under my feet. As an officer of the Conservative Parliamentary Secretariat, I had the advantage of attending, in the official box, the sittings of the House of Commons (in those days, of course, in the House of Lords, since the Commons Chamber had not yet been rebuilt). I found an immensely strong affinity in myself with this institution, an affinity which was to strengthen and to live with me all the days of my life until I was finally bereft of it in 1987. Thus a motivation not initially parliamentary was replaced by a self-sufficient motive, that of becoming and being and remaining a member of that institution.

I want to stress, because I think it gets understressed where the motivation of politicians is discussed, the self-sufficient nature of this motivation. At every stage, from 1947 to 1987, to be and to remain a member of the House of Commons was the overriding and undiscussable motivation of my life as a politician. The attempt to make myself a Member of Parliament, to get there, involved me in talking—first of all at a bye-election in the West Yorkshire coalfield in 1947, and thereafter wherever I could persuade them to listen—to my fellow countrymen in public meetings. So I had to explore, as one not unaccustomed to addressing audiences, though of a different character, the presumptions upon which I addressed my fellow citizens in political meetings. Though I had not yet formulated it as I was later to do, I have no doubt that I was already conscious of the great assumption of the politician addressing his fellow countrymen, namely the identity of introspection, the identity of insight, the suppressed major premise of the syllogism. A politician talks to his fellow men, exhorts his fellow men, instructs his fellow men, upon a common basis which he assumes to exist between him and them, the basis of a common insight, a common self-recognition. He would be bereft of his power to persuade if he could not assume a common dimension, a common background, rarely spelled out but always present in his course of argument. In short, I assumed that my fellow countrymen felt and thought as I did about their own country. It is, stated naked like that, perhaps a startling proposition. Yet I feel sure it underlies most political discourse—the assumption of addressing those who are peers not only in the sense that, of course, by their vote collectively they hold the power to give you what you want or to withhold it, but peers in the sense that they can be addressed upon the basis of common unstated assumptions. That is the major premise from which, by the application of explicit minor premises, all conclusions are drawn in political discourse.

So, here was I in the late 1940s, addressing my fellow countrymen on the assumption that the country I lived in, the country in whose successful self-defence I had participated for six or seven years was also the country in which they lived and about which they felt and thought in the same way that I did. On that basis, I sought and obtained a narrow majority in Wolverhampton South-West in 1950 and began to address another assembly, also an assembly of peers, but in a rather different sense, though still an assembly of peers with this in common: the validity (and it is a most remarkable proposition if you step away from it) of decisions arrived at in that place by a majority is upheld by all who participate. It is the link between that place and those outside who constitute it—the assumption that law is made and authority is exercised by means of a certain procedure gone through in that place and decisions arrived at in that place, however debatably and however narrowly. I had become aware, in other words, of debate, I had discovered that debate in the House of Commons was congenial. It had something in common with the kind of discourse with which I was already familiar; it was a discourse in which peers have to be persuaded. Parliamentary debate is special in this respect: it is debate carried on in the foreknowledge of the end result, but it is debate which nevertheless is carried on for the purpose of affecting the mind and point of view of those addressed upon the assumption of a common basis which they all share, namely, the function and authority of that place, the manner in which it goes about its own business and the validity of the results.

It was an environment so attractive, an environment so congenial to me that I remember distinctly the sensation which I had on each of the three occasions when I refused government office. (By the way, for the record, this well-known 'resigner' resigned only once in all his political career, and that in a junior capacity, though he did in fact decline office three times.) I remember on each occasion the sensation when I re-entered the House of Commons after notifying my decision. It was like coming home to one's mother. It was as though I said, 'I am back again; I am back where I belong, I have not gone away, I am back.'

This congenial nature of the House of Commons, though I believe it was established early, continued to strengthen and deepen its hold on me during the whole of the time that I was a member. If I am asked, as I sometimes am in Sixth Forms, about the motivation of a politician, I tell them 'his real motive is that he wants to remain what he is because he enjoys it, the only justification you will find for doing anything in your life'. I am not sure this is always understood by Sixth Forms, nor always well received by those who instruct Sixth Forms; but at any rate that is the offering which I have to make.

So, here was I by the middle 1950s, with the original grounds on which I had decided to make my life in politics immensely remote, immensely obsolete, but hooked upon a way of life, an all-embracing way of life and one which utilized all my available faculties. It is a paradox all right, but it is a paradox which, when he gets his scalpel out, Professor Skidelsky may even succeed in finding instructive.

I want now to move on from my first point of vantage, (which you remember was in February 1946) and come nearer to modern times with October 1963. In October 1963, Iain Macleod and I, having declined to accept office under Lord Home, were out of office. One's life as a politician, especially as a junior politician, is lived in the presence of what the Romans called the *cursus honorum*, it is lived in the presence of a gradation of achievement, not a gradation of achievement which your essential Member of Parliament would admit to, but a gradation of achievement which is pressed upon them from many quarters. Of course, office is very amusing. It is an amusing exercise of the intellect to take part in the machinery of government and apply one's analytical talents to the content of administration, not to mention legislation. I will not seriously attempt to disclaim having enjoyed office—in the Ministry of Housing and Local Government for just over a year, in the Treasury in 1957 and curiously enough as Minister of Health for three and a quarter years from 1960 to 1963, the longest period I think that anybody was Minister of Health in that meaning of the term. Now all that was over—over for an unforeseeable period. It was as if a spring in my mind snapped back into action. I had lived through years in which the Government to which I belonged had been engaged in the business of attempting to create governmental control over essential prices, including the price of labour. It was the age of Franco-Macmillanite planning, it was the age (the early age) of prices and incomes policy. I had found this profoundly repugnant, repugnant because it jarred with another Tory prejudice, the Tory prejudice that, upon the whole, things are wiser than people, that institutions are wiser than their members and that a nation is wiser than those who comprise it at any specific moment. The notion that there could be vested in

5

ascertainable individuals in government wisdom sufficient to lay out and dispose the effort and resources of society as they expressed themselves in prices was to me deeply repugnant. Now in 1963 I was able to articulate and to explore this prejudice.

I had to reconcile it, of course, with the rest of my political framework, the intellectual framework within which I had been living for fifteen or sixteen years. I found no great difficulty in doing that to my own satisfaction. (One's own satisfaction is the criterion by which one judges intellectual achievement.) To my own satisfaction, I reached the conclusion that the price mechanism is one of the means by which a society takes certain collective decisions in a manner not necessarily ideal, but a manner which is manageable and acceptable and broadly speaking regarded as workable, a mechanism which cannot safely or wisely be replaced by conscious formulation and by compulsion.

So there started a period in which I was formulating to my fellow countrymen the doctrine of the market and following that doctrine as far as it would go in all directions.

I found myself engaging in a fundamental critique of the whole theory of trade unions, since this was the use of coercion in order to produce a different price for an article from that which would otherwise be placed upon it by supply and demand. Thus I found myself drawn into all that intense argument, which was to run on for another twenty years, on the legal basis of the trade unions. I found myself exploring the theory of nationalized industry. I found myself (conveniently) embattled against the Labour Government of the years 1964–1970 and taking my part in providing language for a Conservative Party which received its majority in the 1970 Election as offering propositions recognizably identifiable with what in those days was called 'Selsdon Man'. (The conference held in these early days of 1970 to decide the attitude of the Conservative Party towards prices and incomes policy was held at Selsdon Park.)

I had in fact done a major intellectual job upon my relationship with my political environment and upon my relationship with the public at large and with my own constituents. I had taken them all through it with me and they had found sufficient interest in it to bring me larger audiences during the 1960s than any other politician in or out of government was attracting. It was evidently something they were prepared to examine and on which they were prepared to find some commonality of understanding. Or was I mistaken about that? At any rate, I had re-established and refined the assumed identity of introspection upon which I had always felt that my business as a public man and a representative was to be conducted.

Now I am going to skip over 1968—1968 was not really very important as I will explain in a moment—and move on to my third vantage point, in July 1972. In July 1972, having fought in the country, on the Continent and in the House of Commons the battle against the European Communities Bill and lost—lost only because a guillotine motion was carried with the aid of Liberal votes, but still lost—I had to face the inconceivable. The inconceivable was that, without a wave of public and national resentment, the House of Commons had solemnly and deliberately voted away its historic and essential powers and functions, the unique right to tax, the accepted right to legislate and the undoubted right to call the policies of government to account, the power to demand that the House's confidence should be enjoyed by whoever governed the United Kingdom. All this was part of the universe in which I had lived since the War. The pillars had been removed, but 'earth's foundations stayed' and I had to cope with this shattering event. I drafted a letter, to be sent to the Chancellor of the Exchequer on the last day of that session, applying for appointment to the Chiltern Hundreds, for I did not see how it was possible to continue to belong to a body which had disembowelled itself and disavowed its essential nature. However, it so happened that by 1972 another feature in my intellectual scenery had established itself, another element in my understanding of that common introspection which I presumed. A nation which could support the House of Commons, a nation which could be governed in this way 'godly and quietly', was a nation of such a character that it would accept as law, and as morally binding upon it, what was decided by an elective body, provided always that elective body could periodically be remoulded by it. ('It' is a collective expression which, like all collective expressions, contains an undue admixture of metaphor. But where would we be without metaphor? We would not be talking at all.) The concept, therefore, of a nation which talked and could be talked to and was governable as this nation was governable, depended upon this characteristic—that its members would so identify themselves with one another that the non-existence of a Conservative vote in County Durham or the non-existence of a Labour vote in Hampshire would not render Durham or Hampshire ungovernable as part of the United Kingdom by Labour or Conservative governments. I looked for a word and I did not find a satisfactory word. The only word which I found for working purposes was 'homogeneous', homogeneous in that defined sense, politically homogeneous, capable of perceiving the totality of the nation in such a way as to submit to the will of the totality, given that the totality's will could be altered, influenced and manipulated through the nation's parliamentary institutions. This underlying characteristic of homogeneity was defied by the underlying assumptions of what the nation had done in 1972. There was no such homogeneity between this nation and the other nations of the European Economic Community so long as they were nations at all—if the term 'nation' could be employed in the same way, and the natural assumption was that it *could* be employed in the same way.

Meanwhile, there had been a 'little local difficulty' over the homogeneity of the population of the United Kingdom, the question whether changes in that population did not threaten the eventual survival of political homogeneity. Were there limits of tolerance beyond which homogeneity could not be sacrificed without the whole system, the whole assumption becoming untenable? It was because I had become identified with that question that after 1968 I enjoyed a freedom of expression pretty well unique in the politics of my time—the freedom of a man who does not want anything that those in power can give. There is nothing virtuous about this, because he knows he is not anyhow going to get what he wants: still, he has got the freedom. Such was the freedom, which, after 1968, I enjoyed. I had deployed it in the attempt to convince the nation that in 1972 with the European Communities Act it had done something impossible for it, something which it could not possibly have meant to do. There, I think, lies the significance for me of this third vantage point to which I have asked you to accompany me. At that point I was saying to myself: 'It is true there is this common introspection which I have assumed all along and without which I cannot live and exist as a politician. Therefore they cannot possibly have meant what they have done. Therefore, if I can bring home to them, if events bring home to them, that they did what they did not mean, they will reject it.' In that framework, I have lived my life (I suppose, to an extent, though politically dead, I am still living) to this day, appealing to what must be the implication of a common introspection. The term 'common introspection' is one which I would like to leave as part of my submission. I have seen it used, and this is entirely congenial to me, as part of a definition, indeed perhaps the essential definition, of a nation as those between whom there is a commonality of introspection. At least it comes near to what I am attempting by my unsatisfactory adjective 'homogeneous'.

A politician's life is much more dependent upon faith than it is dependent upon knowledge and belief. For persistence, (which is the same as survival) there has to be a continued faith in the assumptions upon which a political lifetime has been founded. I do not think that I am probably so very different from other politicians—except maybe in being a little more self-analytical—when I say that assumed commonality of introspection between themselves and those whom they represent and those whom they govern lies at the heart of their ability to function and to stay alive.

'Give Richard leave to live till Richard die.' I have been accustomed since June 1987 to refer to myself as a dead man. I have got a sympathy now for the dead that I never had before; when I go through a cemetery, I say to myself 'I know just how they are feeling! They are not there.' The experience that has made me a 'no-man' since June 1987 was that I had no constituency. It was not being no longer a member of the House of Commons, not being debarred from the institution, from the club; it was having no ground on which to stand that convinced me that I had been shot through the head and was living thereafter a kind of ghostly sort of existence. Perhaps it paid me back for the story that I used—I am sure, with tiresome iteration—to tell my constitutents in Wolverhampton and also in South Down, the story of the mythological giant, Antaeus, who could only be overcome if you could lift him off the ground and keep his feet off it for a sufficient length of time. His is the very image of a politician.

Theory and Practice
A Response

ROBERT SKIDELSKY

I am somewhat at a loss to know how to respond. I had Mr Powell's very short abstract of what he intended to say; and we have just heard his eloquent and moving speech. A political columnist wrote just the other day that when Mr Powell lost his seat in the House of Commons it lost its most persuasive speaker; and having just heard him, we can appreciate what he meant. The trouble is, I don't know which of the two, the abstract or speech, to reply to, as they are by no means the same.

Let me start with a passage from the abstract, since this was echoed strongly in Mr Powell's speech. 'Politicians' he wrote 'are professionals who cope with those circumstances which threaten to disturb the *status quo* in a society.' And we have just heard him describe himself as a 'respector of institutions, a respector of monarchy . . . a respector of everything in which authority was capable of being embodied'.

Now it seems that when Mr Powell talks about the professional politician he has in mind a particular kind of politician—himself. For his is not a good description of the professional politician in general. Many professional politicians clearly want to *disturb* the *status quo*. His description fits a certain kind of Conservative (or as he said this afternoon Tory) practice; but not even that of the present Conservative Party, whose 1987 Manifesto promised, rather incongruously, 'to press on with the radical Conservative reforms we embarked on in 1979'. I would not call Mrs Thatcher a *status quo* politician; but perhaps Mr Powell would not consider her to be a Conservative either.

But does Mr Powell's definition of a politician fit even himself? He has often been called the true progenitor of Thatchersim. In the 1960s he went round the country challenging the prevailing 'Franco-Macmillanite' wisdom which certainly represented the *status quo* of that time. In particular he demanded that the price of labour be fixed by the market, and not by government or trade unions.

Now Mr Powell might reasonably reply that it was the Prices and Incomes policy started by Harold Macmillan and continued through the 1960s and 1970s which represented the innovation; and he was merely trying to restore the previous *status quo*. He says that his arguments on this matter were heard with interest and approval by large audiences all over the country. And perhaps on this issue he was truly voicing the 'common introspection'. Incomes policies were never popular except with economists and administrators, and they were discontinued to the general relief after 1979.

But what about the trade unions? Mr Powell was just as adamant that they should play no part in fixing the price of labour. With that relentless logic for which he is famous he argued—I am speaking from memory here—that the British standard of living would have been much higher had trade unions never existed. At any rate, they play no part in Mr Powell's vision of how an efficient economy should work. But trade unions are far from being an innovation. They are institutions of very long standing, certainly capable of exercising authority, and therefore, according to Mr Powell, worthy of the reverence which such institutions should command. Yet they clearly do not command his reverence. Conversely the market system, about which Mr Powell has been wont to speak reverently, is a purely intellectual construction, which really inspires reverence only among some intellectuals. Mr Ian Gilmour is one of many who have pointed out that dogmatic belief in constructs of this kind runs counter to the whole Tory tradition.

No one who heard Mr Powell recently on Desert Island discs can doubt that beneath that classic, syllogistic exterior beats the heart of a romantic, a British romantic. Running through his political career, I suggest, is an unresolved contradiction between the classic and romantic, between the rational and the religious. This contradiction is a central dividing line in politics. It is about whether public affairs should be arranged according to reason or according to tradition. Mr Powell has made of this contradiction a paradox: he romanticizes reason, and intellectualizes romance. How can one make allegiance to the Conservative Party a matter of logic? Yet, as he admits, Mr Powell broke from the Conservative Party without hesitation, when in 1972 it did something it could not logically have done.

But let us take Mr Powell as he sees himself rather than as others might see him. By *status quo* he appears to mean something like the 'traditions of a society', its permanent features, its constitution, rather than the balance of forces which may exist at a particular time. The duty of the politician is to defend and preserve this heritage, to pass it on to the next generation. I was struck by a passage from a speech he delivered at Enniskillen in Northern Ireland, later the scene of more sombre events, on 7 February 1970:

> For years on end politics seemed to concern itself with nothing more than bread and butter, with taxation, with public services, with subsidies, with prices and rents. Then suddenly . . . men find themselves brought face to face again with the ultimate things, with

what all politics is about in the last resort. The scene alters and the depths are opened up.

Politics in the last resort is about the life and death of nations, about what nations are, about how they change, how they grow, how they perish or are destroyed. It is for this that the individuals who compose nations live and died; it is with this that their strongest and deepest emotions and passions are intertwined.

It is not surprising, I think, that Mr Powell should have found his final political home in Northern Ireland, where politics is still about 'ultimate things'; or his final faith in the permanence of the union of Britain and Ulster. And it is easy to see, too, how his most passionate earlier campaigns—against coloured immigration and against Britain's entry into the EEC—fitted his view of politics as about the 'life and death of nations'. Yet these two campaigns failed; and one feels that, sooner or later, Northern Ireland will become more part of the Irish Republic than part of Britain, though the constitutional formula for achieving such a transition is as yet unthought of.

The reasons for Mr Powell's failures as a politician have to do, I think, with his interesting idea of the 'common introspection', 'the common unstated assumptions' to which he says the politician appeals. This is important. Ordinary introspection tells us that being British is more than just a matter of legal identity—having a British passport. It has to do with consciousness of, and pride in, being part of a particular society, of sharing in its common rituals, of worshipping at its common shrines. It is what makes the governance of any society possible. Years ago, Bernard Crick in his book *In Defence of Politics* argued that it is politics which creates commonality, rather than the other way round. I think he was wrong: commonality is what makes politics possible. When it is not there, you have war. The Lebanon today is a grim example, and there are many others.

Having said this, it remains true that politics does not take place at this level of introspection: that which makes politics possible is not what politics is about. When the issue is perceived as involving the 'life and death' of the nation politics stops. Most politicians appeal most of the time to the 'common introspections' of different groups of constituents, and these are chiefly concerned with their material interests. Politics is chiefly about accommodating and harmonizing conflicts of interest. In other words, although it is the existence of a General Will which makes politics possible, politics is about governing divided societies.

On three occasions in his political life, Enoch Powell appealed to the 'common introspection'—to undo the settlement of a non-white population in Britain, to reverse the Act of Parliament which took Britain into the EEC, and to maintain the union between Britain and Northern Ireland. The last issue is not yet resolved; but on the first two occasions Mr Powell clearly failed; and this failure, for better or worse, is now irreversible. His advocacy was compelling; and on both occasions he had much popular support. But neither issue was seen by the 'common introspection' as a 'life and death' issue. Thus neither ousted ordinary politics; and the two party leaderships were able to arrange matters to their own satisfaction.

Mr Powell is unique in postwar politics in his effort to understand the British, and this is what makes him uniquely interesting. Professional politicians set themselves more mundane tasks. I remember a seminar held at Nuffield College, Oxford in the 1960s at which David Butler asked Powell why he went round the country making disturbing speeches. He replied 'I am looking for an echo.' He found one, but it was too weak.

Markets and Morals:
Self, Character and Markets

G. W. SMITH

I

A market may be defined as a set of competitive relationships in which agents strive, within limits set by ground rules, to better their own economic positions, not necessarily at the expense of other people, but not necessarily not at their expense either. A degree of indifference to the market fates of others is, manifestly, an inevitable feature of the market practice, so defined. But though indifference is clearly logically endemic to markets, it has been denied that selfishness is necessarily involved in the raw competition of market activity. Thus, Hayek maintains that market behaviour is not selfish on the grounds that the market is a competitive non zero-sum 'wealth-creating game' in which individuals 'use their own knowledge for their own ends' in a system whose operations, *via* the 'Invisible Hand', also produce unintended benefits for others.[1] But for behaviour to be selfish it clearly need not necessarily disbenefit other people; it is enough that it is pursued, or persisted in, regardless of its effects upon others. And this is precisely what the institutional 'indifference' of market activity amounts to. Admittedly individuals who understand the Hayekian logic of the market know (or believe) that the long-run chances of everyone's benefiting are maximized by acting in a rigorously competitive manner, and so they at least in one sense act with a 'regard for others'. But *ipso facto* this category of market agents has an even stronger reason than the ignorantly selfish for disregarding the *specific* interests of all the *particular* individuals with whom they have economically to do. 'Market selfishness', the disregard for others' market interests, is thus a logically inevitable feature of market activity.

H. B. Acton makes a different point in connection with markets and selfishness. He argues that, even though market activity is admittedly very much a matter of looking after one's own interests and putting them first, this is something which must be clearly distinguished from greed, or avarice, or a callous disregard for the extra-market welfare of

[1] F. A. Hayek, *Law, Legislation and Liberty*, Vol. 2, *The Mirage of Social Justice* (London: Routledge & Kegan Paul, 1982), 153–4.

15

other people. After all, the reasons someone might have for *entering* the market may be very different from the reasons which govern his behaviour *once in*.[2] And this is surely correct. Just as an athelete may compete hard for his country, so an entrepreneur might strive for disinterested or even altruistic ends. There is nothing logically problematical in the thought that a successful market agent might subscribe to a whole range of perfectly respectable non-market values and be, *inter alia,* a charitable neighbour, a loyal friend, and a dutiful citizen. Acton concedes that the quest for profits might become an end-in-itself for some people, but that there is nothing inevitable about this. His view is, then, that there is nothing morally wrong with a competitive striving to further one's market interests and, as an efficient wealth-creating system, the market is justified as the best instrument for supplying the necessary means for furthering any of an indefinite range of non-market ends and values which people may choose to pursue, not to speak of its intimate connection with individual freedom.

This is a tolerably familiar understanding of enterprise and markets, as is the view of critics who castigate it as, basically, a philosophy of selfishness. There is, however, nothing in the Hayek/Acton view of the market to suggest that either market selfishness or greed are in any way especially native or deeply ingrained features of the human personality, or that the market itself is an especially 'natural' institution or practice. On the contrary, market selfishness is presented essentially as a form of social behaviour appropriate to a specific social context, as (so to speak) simply part of the repertoire of a competent social actor. Now competent social actors are, by definition, not only capable of understanding the point of the market practice and of following the rules of the market game, they must also be able to distinguish this game from others, and all games from other ruled-governed but otherwise quite ungamelike activities, e.g., relationships of friendship, charity or citizenship. Hence, if anything is presupposed by this view of markets and market agency it is a widespread capacity for personal autonomy, in the fairly basic sense of an ability to distinguish between contexts and roles and to shift appropriately between them.

For many liberal defenders of the market this conception of the individual as, essentially, an autonomous chooser represents one of the great moral strengths of the system. There is, however, a line of criticism which identifies precisely this aspect as expressive of a basic philosophical inadequacy of market thinking, and one which is, moreover, intrinsically connected with selfishness. Thus, the charge that markets create or encourage selfishness is taken by these critics further

---

[2] H. B. Acton, *The Morals of Markets: an Ethical Exploration* (London: Longman, 1971), 13.

than the elementary *logical* platitude that market indifference is a constitutive feature of competitive market behaviour, but it does not simply amount to the *moral* claim (*contra* Acton) that markets overly stimulate or facilitate the graver vices of greed and callousness, though it often embraces this charge too. The point is rather a *conceptual* one about what is implied for our understanding of selfishness by what these critics take to be a philosophically deficient conception of the agent as an autonomous chooser. It is to an investigation of some aspects of this line of criticism that I wish to devote the remainder of this paper.

II

Jeremy Waldron puts the point in question nicely. According to many critics the liberal individualist way of looking at the self, he says, ' . . . parades [an individual's] social connections as something he can distance himself from, reflect on and therefore bargain for, and it presents the rules and practices constitutive of his community as something to be toyed with and haggled over in the interests of a self that is somehow mysteriously detached from them'.[3] According to Waldron, the pith of the charge against the liberal understanding of the self is that it lacks depth, that it involves a conception of self-identity which is essentially abstract and nebulous, bereft of substantial and meaningful attachments. Liberal agents are thus unable to commit themselves seriously to common projects or to social relationships, or to identify their interests fully with others because, in the last resort, they always conceive of themselves as distinct and detached from others and from their community. (For the liberal, ironically, we may say, there is always much *less* to the individual than meets the eye.) The selfishness to which autonomous market individuals are supposed especially to be prone, therefore, is (as Waldron puts it) 'superficiality'—a superficiality in human relationships arising from superficial understanding of the nature of the self.

Waldron presents this attack on the epistemological underpinnings of liberalism only to conclude that it is mistaken, or at least overdone. He suggests that the capacity to stand back from our commitments from time to time which is involved in the abstraction of the self, and the ability critically to re-consider them in the light of our other priorities and values, does not necessarily mean that we must always be holding something back from them. Clearly he has a point. Indeed, it

---

[3] J. Waldron (ed.), *Nonsense Upon Stilts: Bentham, Burke and Marx on the Rights of Man* (London: Methuen, 1987), 204.

might even sometimes be the case that our depth of commitment is all the greater precisely because we known that we have freely chosen the relationship or the cause, and the obligations which ensue may be all the more exigent upon us because we accept them as being self-imposed. But even so, the psychological mechanisms of commitment or withdrawal may equally well work in the reverse direction and, in any event, Waldron's response perhaps misses the crux of the liberal's difficulties.

The point is that the liberal conception of the abstract and superficial self has been seen, at least by many communitarian and socialist critics, as something which must be grasped in historical and social terms. For them the market is more than simply a social *practice* which furnishes a context in which a certain characteristic pattern of behaviour is elicited. It is also, and more importantly, a social *circumstance*, or *set of circumstances*, which have evolved under specific historical conditions and which have, *pari passu*, produced, perhaps even determined, a distinctive self-understanding in those subjected to its conditions.

L. A. Siedentop formulates a particularly crisp version of this view.[4] According to him, modern society is characterized by the separation of civil society and state, by industrialism and division of labour, and by the spread of market relations. As a result, social roles are multiplied in comparison with earlier forms of society. People are therefore required to take on an ever larger number of social roles and thus come to see themselves as essentially role bearers rather than simply as participants in some specific and limited role. Hence the advent of the modern 'individual', and the appearance of the self which assumes and discards social *persona* without being identical with any of them. Siedentop argues that this development of a sense of individuality ' . . . marks the birth of the will in a peculiarly modern sense—the sense in which the potentialities of the self can never be exhausted in the actual, leaving an abstract "I" over and above social structure'.[5]

From this perspective the superficiality associated by Waldron with liberal selfishness appears much more profound and intractable than he is apparently prepared to allow. The difficulty may be put in this way. The multiplication of social roles, together with the expansion of the market and the associated encroachment upon traditional and custom-

---

[4] 'Political Theory and Ideology: the case of the state', in D. Miller and L. A. Siedentop (eds), *The Nature of Political Theory* (Oxford: Clarendon Press, 1983), 53–73. Hayek presents his own notable evolutionary view of social development, in which he situates the individual in a nexus of social relations—for him too the individual is 'socially produced'. The difference, of course, is that for him the 'abstract individual' of market society is philosophically and ethically unproblematical. See e.g. John Gray, *Hayek On Liberty*, 2nd ed. (Oxford: Blackwell, 1984), esp. Ch. 1.

[5] 'Political Theory and Ideology', 59.

ary affective *gemeinschaft* relationships, results in the establishment of a nexus of social circumstances which, in effect, *define* the modern 'individual'. As agents learn to contract with others on a basis of mutual advantage and on limited terms commitments are narrowly circumscribed and subject to a mutual claiming and exercising of rights. Thus, typically, when agents enter exchange relationships it is rarely without a thought for the possibility or even likelihood of exiting on the prospect of a better deal. Market relationships are thus of their nature instrumental and temporary—the result of the coincidental interests of essentially mutually detached agents. In the light of this, and given the historical expansion of the market (and hence of market attitudes), not to speak of the multiplication of social roles claimed by Siedentop, it may well be thought that the prospect of agents resisting the pressure to regard their social connections as something (as Waldron puts it) to be 'haggled' and 'bargained' over in the interests of an abstract self essentially detached from all of them is pretty unrealistic.

It is certainly so regarded by Marxists. Thus, in an influential book amongst radicals and Marxists, Evgeny Pashukanis argues that the market, understood as a system of commodity exchange, rests upon an extensive practice of voluntary contractual agreement between legal parties who must be characterized in abstract terms because the smooth and continuous operations of the market require a set of conditions which enable reciprocal agreements to be made which are clearly definable and generally and easily enforceable by legal authorities.[6] Hence, claims Pashukanis, the inevitability within the market system of the appearance of the abstract individual, the autonomous bearer of individual rights (especially of course the right to own property), assumed to be self-interested, free to engage with others on the basis of reciprocity, and taken to be capable of legal responsibility for his acts and omissions. In other words, the abstract individual, the liberal paradigm of the person, is by no means a natural phenomenon; neither are his credentials grounded in any objective moral imperative. On the contrary, his identity is merely the result of a set of stipulations embedded in practices required for the uninterrupted functioning of a system of market exchanges. A system which, in the opinion of Marxists, has its rationale in the exploitation of wage labour and the relentless pursuit of profits.

Capitalism, and especially the market in wage-labour, must therefore be abolished and society, and hence the self, reconstructed. Pashunkanis's proposals in respect of the new 'communist man', however, amount to nothing more than a disappointingly familiar rehash of

---

[6] E. V. Pashukanis, *Law and Marxism: a General Theory*, C. Arthur (ed.) (London: Ink Links, 1978), esp. Ch. 4.

Enlightenment materialism, according to which society is to be engineered and managed for beings who are merely 'creatures of circumstance', incapable of choice, and thoroughly submerged in their social conditions. It is impossible to avoid the conclusion that, in Pashukanis's communism, men are made social only at the cost of the complete abolition and sacrifice of individual autonomy. There are clues in Marx's own writings, however, which suggest a philosophically more interesting and, on the face of it at least, more attractive alternative.

In the *Grundrisse, à propos* of our understanding of the relation between the individual and society, Marx remarks that 'Society does not consist of individuals, but expresses the sum of inter-relations, the relations within which these individuals stand'.[7] Unfortunately, he never expands to much effect on this but the idea seems to be that the 'common sense' opposition between individuals on the one hand and society on the other is inadequate or misleading because, understood correctly, society consists neither simply of *individuals* (the liberal mistake) nor of *social relations* (the Idealist heresy), but rather of individuals *in* social relations. The individual thus occupies a determinate position in a network of relations which constitute society on the one side and himself as a social individual on the other. This thoroughly 'dialectical' interpenetration of self and society may indeed be thought to furnish the implicit ontological basis upon which Marx grounds his distinctive views about man's essentially *gemeinwesen* nature. But it raises the immediate problem of how, on this account, self is distinguished from society, that is to say, how the individual self can be *both* autonomous *and* substantially social. On this Marx is, again, unfortunately silent. It is, however, possible to venture a rough reconstruction of a possible position here—and to note its fatal inadequacy.

For Marx, perhaps the key difference between capitalism and communism is that, whereas in the former an individual's social relations are, so to speak, chosen for him by the contingencies of the class system, in the latter he will be in a position to choose his own. In class societies, says Marx, 'social relationships take on an independent existence . . . the individual's position in life and his personal development are assigned to him by his class and he becomes subsumed under it'.[8] Thus in one sense individuals are submerged in capitalist society, but in another, because their social relationships are pervaded by the market, they are abstracted and projected above society by their participation in the characteristic conception of self-identity embedded in the social

[7] K. Marx, *Grundrisse* (Harmondsworth, Penguin, 1973), 265.
[8] K. Marx and F. Engels, *The German Ideology*, C. Arthur (ed.) (New York: International Publishers, 1970), 83 and 82.

circumstances in which they exist. They experience autonomy, but an autonomy of an illusory and alienated kind. In contrast, Marx claims that in communism social relations will cease to be coercive and persons will participate in the community as genuine individuals, rather than as involuntary members of a class. That is to say, they will enjoy autonomy in the profound sense of being in the position for the first time in history to choose their social relations rather than having them determined for them by the contingencies of their class positions. Moreover, these relations will also be such as to enable them to experience a genuine depth in their social connections with others, not in the least part because, being non-market relations, they will be unalienated and non-exploitative.

However, apart from making the immense and entirely gratuitous assumption that post-revolutionaries will not want or choose to preserve market relations in some form or other, the programme appears to verge upon incoherence. For, whereas for liberal individualists there is at least logically no problem with the idea that individuals can choose their own relationships—they merely adopt and discard *persona* as they wish—once the Marxian thesis as to the basically social nature of self-identity is annexed to the idea that involuntary social relations must be abolished in communism, any coherent notion of an enduring individual self with a past and a future seems immediately to evaporate. After all, on the basis of the principles of the *Grundrisse*, Marx's ambition must be to enable people to step out of inhibiting social roles without thereby stepping out of society, for, if social relations as such are abolished the social individual, who owes his identity to them, will surely vanish with them. On the other hand, given that social relations must persist in communism (though radically transformed) and people are able to choose which ones to establish, then we have to make sense of the idea of individuals who create their own identity by acts of social choice. Yet, once again, the individual seems immediately to disappear, for how can they intelligibly be said to *endure* as selves through a series of changing relationships which *constitute* them as individuals? The consequence of eliminating the abstract self of liberalism, whilst preserving or enhancing autonomy of choice seems, ironically, to be the complete evaporation of any coherent conception of self-identity, the disappearance of the individual *per se*.

III

Given that the Marxism critique of liberal market man is itself vitiated by profound conceptual difficulties, is there any other way of responding to the charge expressed by Waldron that markets cultivate an attitude of selfish superficiality amongst the generality of market practitioners? Perhaps the first point that is worth making here is that the liberal tradition of thinking on markets and human nature is, of course, by no means a uniform or monolithic one. Indeed, the notion of the market as a game-like practice played by abstract market agents is, if anything, somewhat marginal to an important foundational strand of economic liberalism which stretches from Adam Smith to J. S. Mill. In this tradition the market is squarely seen as a set of social circumstances with a history which conditions the dispositions and attitudes of individuals. But whereas with Marx social conditions are regarded as penetrating to the core of personality and as actually defining self-identity, the liberal utilitarian view of the impact of society on the individual is less radical, in large part because a crucial theoretical distinction is asserted between self and character on the one hand, and between both of these and market circumstances on the other.

Thus, consider what Smith has to say about the virtue of honesty in connection with market circumstances:

> Whenever commerce is introduced into any country, probity and punctuality always accompany it. These virtues in a rude and barbarous country are almost unknown. Of all the nations in Europe, the Dutch, the most commercial, are the most faithful to their word. The English are more so than the Scotch, but much inferior to the Dutch . . . There is no natural reason why an Englishman or a Scotchman should not be as punctual in performing agreements as a Dutchman. It is far more reducible to self interest, that general principle which regulates the actions of every man, and which leads men to act in a certain manner from views of advantage, and is as deeply implanted in an Englishman as a Dutchman.[9]

Smith assumes that we are all uniformly and invariably motivated by 'self-love' or self-interest, and that differences of character are explicable in terms of the interplay between self-interest and variable circumstances. As success in the market requires a reputation for reliability, the more pervasive the market, as in Holland, the more widespread and deeply ingrained in character the necessary virtues of honesty and punctuality. Differences of capacity and skill are explained in basically the same way. Where there is little division of labour, as in 'rude and barbarous' nations, there, says Smith, we always find 'the greatest uniformity of character'. Hence it is differences of occupation which

---

[9] A. Smith, *Lectures on Jurisprudence*, R. L. Meek *et al.* (eds) (Indianapolis: Liberty Press, 1982), 538. Smith's apparently self-depreciatory reference to the Scots loses its irony in the light of the vital difference for him between feckless Highland clansmen and canny Lowlanders like himself.

explain differences of 'genius' rather than as is commonly believed, *vice versa*—the difference between a porter and a philosopher at the age of four or five is, he says, negligible, it is when they come to be employed in their respective occupations that 'their views widen and differ by degrees'.[10] Thus, division of labour, together with the institution of private property and the practice of competitive market exchange, maximizes productive efficiency and general utility, and in the process elicits from self-interested market agents the functionally appropriate virtues, such as honesty and punctuality, as well as producing the differentiated abilities of the porter and the philosopher.

What is particularly of significance to us about this immensely elegant and influential theory is that Smith counters the centrifugal tendencies of self-interest and market competition by harnessing them to the establishment of a set of steady dispositions of an appropriate and socially useful kind, i.e. to a particular kind of *character*. It might be thought, however, that although it is ingenious as an account of the social construction of character it remains ultimately too self-regarding to produce the necessary moral depth described by Waldron.

Two points may be made about this. Firstly, it has to be significant that Smith sees self-interest in a very different light from either the defenders or the critics of the conception of the relation between self and markets with whom we have been concerned so far. For him self-interest generates and sustains significant aspects of a social structure which serves also to discipline the individual into functional social responsibilities, whilst preserving the self's essential autonomy. This is the significance of the introduction of the notion of character as an intermediary between self and market circumstances. Take punctiliousness as a case in point. As a virtue of character, punctiliousness implies a strong and more or less habitual disposition to perform one's contracts and a willingness to admit responsibility for one's failures when one is prevented from doing so, even if the circumstances that prevent one are such that they might plausibly be invoked by a less rigorous character in exculpation, or at least in mitigation of one's behaviour. True, this might not represent the whole of what is required by the idea of 'moral depth', but it is manifestly a long way from the superficiality of the free-floating and abstract self promoted by advocates of the 'market game' and deplored by its critics.

Secondly, it is a mistake (although historically an immensely influential one) to read Smith as grounding either his theory of society or his understanding of the individual simply in self-interest. Thus, Amartya Sen charges the disciples of Smithian self-interest economics with never really progressing beyond Smith's famous comment that we do

---

[10] *Lectures on Jurisprudence*, 493.

not appeal to the benevolence of the butcher, the brewer and the baker for our dinner, but rather to their self-interest. Sen points out that, far from resting economic salvation upon self-interest *per se*, Smith explicitly rejects the view that it is grounded in any single motivation.[11] As for the famous comment upon the butcher and the baker, he maintains very plausibly that Smith's defence of self-interested behaviour is specific rather than general, related to contemporary barriers which Smith believed hampered production, and that he is doing no more here than simply illustrate the terms upon which normal market transactions are carried out in the context of a discussion of the implications of the division of labour.[12] What Smith does not do is simply to identify market relations with the totality of social relations.

Sen's line of argument is taken a step further by Russell Nieli.[13] Nieli contends that Smith in fact conceives of market actors as members of intimate primary groups rather than as abstracted selves, and that he regards the market as a quite narrowly drawn sphere involving only those relations between persons who are not otherwise intimately related. Consequently, Smith assumes that self-interest will frequently, and quite properly, be discounted, as for example within the family group or with intimate friends. And even beyond these intimate groupings Smith identifies a distinct 'order in which individuals are recommended to our beneficence', including more distant relations, benefactors, esteemed colleagues, good neighbours and, at the outermost extreme of intimacy, our countrymen and our nation.

The interpretations offered by Sen and Nieli may be brought interestingly to bear upon Smith's position on self, character and the market. The most obvious way in which obligations of beneficence might be thought to be discharged is by the individual being encouraged, *qua* market agent, to 'run as hard as he can and strain every nerve and every muscle, in order to out strip all his competitors' and being required to reserve his beneficence for strictly extra-market acts of friendship or charity. This of course represents the competitive market actor position promoted by Hayek and Acton. It undoubtedly fits in neatly with Smith's 'Invisible Hand' explanation of economic progress and, a factor perhaps crucial for the whole programme of 'scientific' economics, it preserves the conceptual simplicity of the theory—outside the market the individual may behave as his impulses or the moral circumstances demand, but within the market his behaviour, as *homo economicus*, is motivationally simple, reliable, readily comprehensible and therefore

---

[11] A. K. Sen, *On Ethics and Economics* (Oxford: Blackwell, 1987), 24.

[12] Sen, *On Ethics and Economics*, 23–5.

[13] R. Nieli, 'Spheres of Intimacy and the Adam Smith Problem', *Journal of the History of Ideas*, XLVII (1986), 611–24.

predictable. When methodological imperatives of this kind are combined with individualistic political commitments they produce a potent ideological mix which has historically been very difficult effectively to challenge.[14]

On the other hand, if (as Smith holds) raw market exchange is morally out of place in the intimate spheres of family and close friendship because of considerations of affection and beneficence, then this raises the interesting possibility that the quality of market relationships in contiguous spheres might properly be seen to be coloured by similar, but, of course, correspondingly diluted, moral considerations. Market relationship in their pure form, relationships grounded *solely* in market selfishness, would then be socially much more peripheral, applying only, so to speak, between 'consenting strangers'. Just how far Smith intends considerations of intimacy in fact to stretch is undoubtedly a knotty exegetical question and one which it is not strictly necessary to pursue here. It is sufficient to note that although advocates of the market such as Hayek regard the existence, or persistence, of such essentially *gemeinschaft* factors within economic relationships as irrational and even immoral—as remnants of the closed tribal society within the modern Great Society, the effect of this reading of Smith is considerably to complicate not only the project of a 'science' of economics but also the picture of the individual's understanding of the relation between his interests and his commitments *even within the market itself*, and hence to carry with it what might be thought to be a much more weighty sense of self-identity. It implies, so to speak, a shift in the centre of gravity of the self, from a notion of self-identity as essentially abstract and detached to a significantly more substantial one in which the self is grounded *qua* character in a network of intersecting and overlapping relationships involving a complex set of dispositions of affection, beneficence and obligation, together with an admixture of a more or less qualified kind of individual self-interest.

The 'spheres of intimacy' doctrine, however significant it might be in serving to correct the interpretative perspective on Smith is, however, clearly a recessive element in his thought. Apart from some brief but celebrated comments upon the stupefying effects of the extended division of labour on detail workers Smith shows little awareness of the psychic impact of the market on the individual, nor indeed of the immense expansionary dynamic of capitalism. It was left to early nineteenth century critics of developing capitalism to lament the capacity of the market to encroach upon and to adulterate, if not even entirely to displace, the kinds of spheres of intimacy identified by Smith. In this connection John Stuart Mill is typically regarded as

---

[14] See Sen, *On Ethics and Economics*, Ch. 1 *passim*.

being on the side of the market, as a defender of individual choice and personal autonomy against the conservatism of the likes of Coleridge and Carlyle. But Mill no less than Smith has suffered from a certain retrospective stereotyping. Mill's position may be read, like that of his great predecessor, as being a good deal less categorical than this picture suggests. I want therefore to finish by bringing together some of Mill's thoughts on our theme in the belief that he develops some of the neglected aspects of Smith's thinking, as well as representing perhaps the best expression of the utilitarian liberal compromise between unqualified market individualism and anti-market socialism.

IV

Mill, of course, presents himself as an exponent of 'individuality'. Individualists, in the Millian sense, are those who are capable of making their own lives, of deciding for themselves the kind of person they want to be rather than allowing it to be decided for them by others. And they do this, more often than not, in opposition to custom and against the pressures of social conformity.[15] However, this does not mean that Mill does not acknowledge the importance of established character, on the contrary, as Berger shows, he insists upon it.[16] By character Mill means 'trained dispositions of feeling, desire and action'; but he also maintains that we ourselves must inculcate these dispositions, or at least have a role in so doing. Indeed, Berger points out that in *On Liberty* Mill goes so far as to say that a person whose desires and impulses are not 'his own', in the sense of flowing from a character which he has had a hand in making, does not, strictly speaking, really have a character at all.[17] Moreover, in a recent devastatingly hostile critique, John Gray charges Mill with, in effect, trivialising individuality precisely by neglecting the importance of custom and tradition.[18] According to Gray, individuality is in no way dependent upon distancing or detaching oneself from society, nor upon the process of conducting personal 'experiments in living' designed to discover the 'unique quiddity' Mill apparently believes to lie hidden in each individual. On the contrary, claims Gray, it involves having the good fortune

[15] The *locus classicus* is, of course, Ch. 3 of *On Liberty*.

[16] F. R. Berger, *Happiness, Justice and Freedom: the Moral and Political Philosophy of J. S. Mill* (Berkeley: University of California Press, 1984), 17–19.

[17] *Happiness, Justice and Freedom*, 17.

[18] J. N. Gray, 'Mill's and Other Liberalisms', in K. Haakonssen (ed.), *Traditions of Liberalism: Essays on Locke, Smith and J. S. Mill* (St Leonards, NSW: Centre for Independent Studies, 1988), 119–41, esp. section 3.

to live in a culturally pluralistic society exhibiting a diversity of con-
trasting, interweaving and overlapping traditions and ways of life
which furnish the concrete context out of which our distinct individual
identities arise, as much by chance as by choice. Mill's conception of the
relation between the individual and society is, charges Gray, simply an
abstract and rationalistic fiction.

As a stricture upon Mill's position as we find it in *On Liberty* this is
probably just, if somewhat severe. But it is worth bearing in mind that
Mill is often at his most rhetorical and exaggerated in the celebrated
Essay and his considered doctrine is better sought elsewhere, particularly in those places where he responds to the self-interest philosophy of the professed disciples of Adam Smith, especially his father.

Mill's reaction to the debacle which followed upon James Mill's
attempt in *On Government* to generalize what he takes to be the
Smithian explanatory model, and to present self-interest as the basis of
representative government, is to charge his father with what he calls
'geometrical reasoning'—the fallacy (avoided as we have seen by Smith
himself) of postulating a single factor account of the entirety of human
behaviour.[19] Mill's response is that this constitutes far too narrow a
basis upon which to reason adequately. He shows himself to be more
drawn to the extreme environmentalism of Robert Owen, according to
which the supposedly pre-social or 'natural' self-interest upon which
the market rests is merely the result of corrupting social circumstances,
primary amongst which, of course, is the market itself. Mill never goes
this far himself. That is to say, he never claims that man is a mere
'creature of circumstances' and that social conditions alone are sufficiently powerful to create selfishness. Consequently he never envisages
that the abolition of the market could ever expunge it. Indeed, he thinks
that it would be undesirable even if it were possible—he thoroughly
rejects Comte's vision of a society organized around the creation of
systematic altruism as an attack upon the integrity of the individual. On
the other hand, he is equally decisive in rejecting the idea that society at
large should be modelled upon the market. His considered position is
that self-interest is by no means the pre-social invariable to which his
father held that all social arrangements must be accommodated. It is a
basic human disposition, but one which may be accentuated or dimin-
ished by altering social conditions. Mill believes that an unreformed or
unlimited capitalist market encourages a surplus of unjustifiable self
interest, and with it, crass materialism. Hence the need in his opinion
both to restrict the scope of the market and to moderate, to some degree

---

[19] J. S. Mill, *System of Logic, Collected Works*, J. M. Robson (ed.)
(Toronto: Toronto University Press, 1969), Vol. 8, Book 6 *passim*.

the least, the selfish competitiveness characteristic of raw market relationships.

The philosophical postition lying behind these proposals is crucial to grasping his considered position. As we have seen, Mill holds that if our desires and actions are really to be 'ours' they must flow from a character that is 'ours' too. And, as Berger points out, Mill thinks that this is possible only if we can ourselves take a hand in the creation of our own character, and in this way be at least in part responsible for it, and hence for the desires and actions which flow from it. Indeed, for Mill, unless we can do this we cannot *really* be 'free'.[20] Mill's solution is to argue that we find no difficulty with the idea that we can change other people's characters: we do it all the time by such means as education, persuasion and generally by altering their circumstances by putting them in situations to which they then respond by developing the kinds of qualities and dispositions we are looking for in them. And what we can do for others, we can do for ourselves. Just as we are able to alter other people's characters if we wish, so we can alter our own by simliar means. Social circumstances which are beyond our personal control will, of course, be responsible for much of what we are, but we can nevertheless take a hand in the modification or amendment of our own character, if we wish to do so. And if we do, we then make it, and hence the desires and actions which express it, to that degree, 'our own'.

Thus, on the one hand, character is a matter of 'trained dispositions of feeling, desire and action' and self, on the other, is represented by the wish or the desire to change or to alter a particular disposition or set of dispositions. There is clearly a sense, then, in which, on Mill's model, the self is abstract—given its assigned function, it logically must be analytically distinct from character, and hence itself without character. But, to the degree that an individual actually succeeds in making his character what he wants or wishes it to be, he comes to own, or identify with, his character. Hence self and character are in this respect, uni-fied, and self is informed with character. (We may say that the self is 'encharactered'.) The abstraction of self is thus necessarily qualified and essentially incomplete. In addition, though Mill admittedly abstracts self from *character*, at least in the partial manner just described, he by no means abstracts and projects it beyond *social circumstances*. Quite the contrary. As an empiricist and determinist he is committed to rejecting any idea that the desire for self-change might arise from a contra-causal act of will. He insists that the crucial impulse in the programme of character self-development, namely the actual

[20] For a discussion of the connection between character, freedom and virtue in Mill's 'proof' of human freedom in a deterministic world, see my 'The Logic of J. S. Mill on Liberty' *Political Studies*, xxviii (1980), 232–52.

desire to engage in the process, 'comes from outside or not at all'. Hence the vital necessity asserted in *On Liberty* for 'freedom, and variety of situations', for without the external stimulus provided by individual and social diversity, individuals cannot be expected even to take the first step in making their characters their own, viz. come to conceive the desire to do so.

With these distinctions in mind we may now return to Gray's criticisms. It is undeniably the case that in *On Liberty* Mill's emphasis upon individuality often seems to amount to not much more than character self-change for change's sake, and he may fairly be charged with bending towards a kind of shallow bohemian eccentricity. He may equally be accused of grossly underestimating the importance of tradition, custom and convention in preserving social variety in a pluralistic society, and hence, as Gray argues, of neglecting the very conditions which undergird the possibility of individuals engaging in any project of character self-reform. But Mill's failure here, although undoubtedly giving rise historically to a defective view of liberal values, is surely fundamentally one of balance and emphasis, rather than of principle. For, as has been argued, his considered understanding of the individual is one of a self constitutively informed by character, and of both self and character as thoroughly embedded in a social nexus. And this is perhaps no more apparent than in his treatment of the individual in his market circumstances.

In his *Principles of Political Economy* Mill objects strongly to what he calls 'the most conspicuous and vehment part of the Socialists' teaching: their declamations against competition'.[21] Socialists, he maintains, do not understand competition: 'One of their greatest errors is to charge upon competition all the economical evils which at present exist.' But, where there is no competition, inevitably there is monopoly, and monopoly is nothing other than 'a tax on the industrious for the support of indolence'. Socialists forget that competition cheapens articles and that it can raise as well as lower wages. Mill admits that there are 'inconveniences' to competition, and moral objections to it as a source of jealousy and hostility amongst workers. But if it brings evils, it prevents greater ones. For Mill one of the greatest evils of monopoly is the deleterious effect it has upon character:

> It is a common error of Socialists to overlook the natural indolence of mankind; their tendency to be passive, to be the slaves of habit, to persist indefinitely in a course once chosen. Let them once attain any state of existence which they consider tolerable and they will thenceforth stagnate; will not exert themselves to improve, and by letting

---

[21] J. S. Mill *Principles of Political Economy, Collected Works*, J. M. Robson (ed.) (Toronto University Press, 1965), Vol. 3, 794.

their faculties rust, lose even the energy required to preserve them from deterioration. Competition may not be the best conceivable stimulus, but it is at present a necessary one, and no one can foresee the time when it will not be indispensible to progress'.[22]

In effect, then, competition is the market analogue of the 'freedom and variety of situations' of *On Liberty*—it is a necessary social stimulus to the realization of that vital interest we all share as 'progressive beings' in character self-development.

This does not mean, of course, that Mill neglects the importance of competition for productivity and economic efficiency generally, but it does entail the ultimate subordination of these economic values to the non-economic end of character self-development. Thus he is prepared to set strict limits to the scope of competition, rejecting it categorically in the particular form of competition between capital and labour, not so much because it involves competition between workers for jobs (although, as we have seen, he deplores the 'jealousy and hostility' that this can encourage), but more on the grounds that the typical relation between employer and worker is inconsistent with the improvement of the characters of working people. In this respect Mill regards the market as being positively debilitating upon character (not unlike the effects of monopoly), in that being in employment means, essentially, being in a state of dependency, having one's working hours taken from under one's own control and placed in the hands of others—managers, foremen and the like. The effect, Mill argues, cannot be other than to inhibit any growth of a sense of personal independence and effectiveness, and to engender practical and intellectual passivity. Hence his advocacy of workers associations, in which producers will own their own means of production, and all will participate in the joint management and direction of their enterprises—for enterprises they must remain, being required to compete with rival associations in the market.[23]

Thus, whereas Smith tends to see the connection between character and market in functional terms—market circumstances 'producing' the appropriate market character (*vide* punctiliousness), and the point of the system and practice being (certainly in the eyes of most of his self-professed disciples) the individual pursuit of economic advantage—Mill understands it quite differently. For him the market is but one aspect of a complex of social circumstances, the organization and arrangement of which must ultimately be subordinated to an overriding non-economic end, namely the establishment of conditions designed to

---

[22] Ibid., 795.
[23] Ibid., Vol. 3, Book 4, Ch. 7.

stimulate individuals to the achievement of freedom, understood in Mill' strong sense of character self-development.

It might be objected that there is nothing here that really distinguishes Mill's position from the Hayek/Acton view of market relationships. That is to say, they remain essentially instrumental, a means by which individuals pursue their own private satisfactions, in this case personal self-realization, and hence 'superficial'. Certainly, Mill often seems to equate 'making one's own character' with 'making one's own character different from everyone else's', especially when discussing individuality, and this seems clearly to imply a somewhat instrumental or conditional view of social relationships—here the emphasis is primarily upon the need for an opportunity to exit from cramping relationships in the name of freedom and originality. But even in *On Liberty*, where this kind of talk is most prominent, Mill qualifies it with the 'no harm to others' condition, and this of course includes respect for the rights of others. In the economic writings there is much less stress on individuality as such. Instead Mill's concern is to reorganize the market to combat passivity, to encourage the realization of capacities and powers rather than letting them 'rust'. And, clearly in response to the kinds of fears expressed by both conservative and socialist critics of the market as to the tendency of a rapidly expanding capitalist economy to erode shared moral commitments and to displace *gemeinschaft* relationships, Mill places particular emphasis upon the aspect of moral responsibility and social solidarity in character self-development.

Thus ownership is itself held to be character building. Proprietorship, says Mill, exercises 'an improving influence', and (scarcely 'bohemian') it helps inculcate 'the moral virtues of prudence, temperance and self-control'.[24] Moreover ownership in the form of industrial co-operation encourages a sense of mutual interdependence and social responsibility, ultimately not only between the members of a co-operating workforce but in society more generally.[25] And all this Mill expects to occur anyway in the context of a gradual decline in the rate of industrial expansion and a corresponding moderation in the intensity of economic competition as we approach the inevitable 'stationary state'.[26]

It is, of course, not difficult to disparage this rather rosy scenario, particularly with our advantage of hindsight. Mill was writing at a time

[24] Ibid., Vol. 2, Book 3, Ch. 7, sections. 2 and 3.
[25] Ibid., Vol. 3, Book 4.
[26] 'I confess I am not charmed with the ideal of life held out by those who think that the normal state of human beings is that of struggling to get on; that the trampling, crushing, elbowing, and treading on each other's heels, which form the existing type of social life, are the most desirable lot of human kind, or anything but the disagreeable symptoms of one of the phases of industrial progress.' (Ibid., Vol. 3, 754.)

of immense economic and social change, before the structure of the modern industrial state had imposed itself, and in an atmosphere of broad social speculation. Although Gray is undoubtedly right in his accusation that Mill's handling of the whole question of the institutional preconditions of economic growth is analytically unimpressive and represents a regression from Smith and earlier classical economists, it is surely a mistake, and an important one, simply to dismiss Mill as a utopian dreamer, a self-indulgent and short-sighted advocate of a socially irresponsible narcissistic egoism.[27] For this involves a failure to appreciate the depth of the moral perspective that Mill applies to the phenomenon of the modern market.

Not everyone of course has qualms about the rise of the moral dominance of the model of the abstract market individual, whose style is typically to construe social relationships simply in terms (to use Waldron's phrase) of 'the interests of a self that is somehow mysteriously detached from them'—the immense influence of Hayek's thought manifestly attests to its impact. But for anyone who has worries about a conception of personality which projects the self beyond all of its social connections, and yet who may also be repelled (politically and/or intellectually) by the Marxian alternative, according to which the self is either completely submerged in society or fragmented into a congeries of social relations, the liberal utilitarianism of Smith and Mill may well have its legitimate appeal. For the tripartite analysis advanced by both thinkers (self–character–circumstances) surely captures, particularly in Mill's version of the theory, the essentially ambiguous location of the self. That is to say, it at least takes seriously, and attempts to satisfy, the *contending* moral demands of independence and commitment. Applied to market circumstances it grounds a conception of market relationships according to which the market is not simply seen as a competitive game played by abstract individuals which necessarily excludes or marginalizes non-market values. On the contrary, it implies a system of social relationships, the ultimate point of which is to subserve the interests (and needs) of substantial, 'encharactered', persons. This is not the time to enter into a discussion of the broad implications of this view, but one negative point may be made. It is an understanding which finds at least part of its strength and moral attractiveness in ruling out absolutely any defence of market selfishness which appeals to the principle that pretty well anything goes because the market is really nothing but a rat race.

[27] Gray, 'Mill's and Other Liberalisms', 130–2.

Markets and Morals*
A Response

DON LOCKE

The major merit claimed for markets is that they are the most efficient mechanism known to us for providing people with what they want. By 'markets' or 'the market' I mean the theory and practice of the free market economy; I shall sometimes also speak of 'the market economy' and 'the market ideology', but only for the sake of variety. The idea is that, left to themselves, the laws of supply and demand will always see to it that people eventually get the best possible product at the best possible price.

This has of course been disputed. There are those who have urged the superiority of a planned or controlled economy. But at the moment the defenders of the market seem to be winning hands down, and in some most unexpected places. I cannot help wondering, myself, whether this is not just a fashion, whether in another forty years we won't be rediscovering the merits of planning and control. But let us accept the economic efficiency of markets, if only for the sake of argument. Our topic is not their economic merit but their moral virtue.

Thus some will insist that, for all their economic advantages, markets are a force for evil, encouraging selfishness, greed, competitiveness and a mean and grasping conception of human nature. And some will insist that so far from being immoral, or amoral, markets are in fact a force for good, as a defence of autonomy, liberty, equality, and right conduct. In this paper I shall attempt a review of six of the most prominent arguments in this debate, three on each side. I shall not come to any definite conclusions, because personally I do not find any of these arguments persuasive, let alone conclusive.

Selfishness and Greed

The most obvious objection to markets is that they encourage selfishness and greed, and that that's a bad thing. The second half of this

* Geoffrey Smith has substantially rewritten his paper for this volume, to the extent that the reply which I gave at the conference is no longer relevant. I have therefore written my reply, to the extent that it is no longer a reply. Instead I discuss, very sketchily, some of the background issues, in order to provide a context for Geoffrey Smith's more careful and more detailed discussion.

argument seems hard to resist. Admittedly, there are some so over-whelmed by the other merits of markets that they are willing to insist that if markets encourage selfishness and greed then, in that case, greed is good. But this seems a desparate measure. The crucial, contentious, issue is whether markets do encourage selfishness and greed, and if so, how.

I can think of three suggestions: that markets assume selfishness and greed; that markets rely on selfishness and greed; and that markets reward selfishness and greed. But notice first that selfishness and greed are not quite the same thing, and that both are different from self-interest. If I eat as much as I can hold, and more, when no-one else wants any, that is greedy without being selfish; if desperately hungry, I eat my sandwiches without sharing them with others who are equally hungry, that is selfish without being greedy; and if I take pains to follow a good diet for the sake of my health, that is self-interested, because in my interests, without being either selfish or greedy. Moreover, what-ever may be the case about selfishness and greed, self-interest, as such, is not immoral. On the contrary, under the name of prudence, it has often been regarded as a virtue.

This may seem to give the defender of markets an easy reply to the objection; what markets depend on, and therefore encourage, he may say, is not selfishness and greed but self-interest, which is a different, and more respectable, matter. But this reply is to easy. Self-interest, selfishness and greed may be different, but they can and do overlap: the pursuit of self-interest can become selfishness, when it involves ignor-ing or over-riding the interests of others; in some forms, carried to extremes, it can even become greed. So if it is conceded that markets encourage self-interest, it would seem to follow that they will also encourage selfishness and greed in those cases where selfishness and greed happen to be (or are thought to be) in our interests. The reference to self-interest is therefore an irrelevance, and we need not enquire whether markets encourage or promote it. Our topic is selfishness and greed, whether in our interests or not.

The first suggestion was that markets assume selfishness and greed. That is, the market ideology takes it for granted that human beings are selfish and greedy by nature, and builds its economics on that assump-tion. Yet this seems at first sight a factual objection, not a moral one, and one which can safely be left to look after itself. If the market ideology assumes that people are selfish and greedy when they are not, then markets will not function, or will not function as well as they should. Or conversely, the fact that markets function as well as they do, should be evidence that the underlying assumption about human nature are sound. But either way it is a matter of fact, which we might want to lament, but cannot turn into a moral objection.

Things are not quite so simple. With human psychology, assuming that something is so can help to make it so: the easiest way to be happy or in love is to believe that you are. So by assuming that people are selfish and greedy, the market ideology may help to make them so. This objection is a moral objection after all. But is it in fact correct? Does the market have to assume that people are selfish and greedy? Only, it seems to me, if the market economy actually requires selfishness and greed. That is, the only reason I can see why the market ideology should want to assume selfishness and greed is that the market economy relies on selfishness and greed, in that without them it would not function properly. And even then the marketeer is not obliged to assume selfishness and greed. On the contrary he may want to insist that, unfortunately, people are not selfish and greedy enough, which is why markets do not work as well in practice as in theory they might.

So if there is an objection here, it seems to turn into the second suggestion, that markets rely on selfishness and greed. Whether they assume it or not is beside the point; the objection is that, however much people may or may not be greedy, the market economy wants them to be, so that it can function the more effectively. But I am not sure whether this is true either. The point, presumably, is that the efficiency of the market depends on people, both sellers and buyers, being willing to drive the hardest bargain possible; and this in turn seems to require selfishness and greed, the desire of the seller to sell dear, and of the buyer to buy cheap. But this is true only if the efficiency of the market is measured solely in monetary terms. Suppose that traders in the market are driven by desires other than the desire to drive the hardest bargain possible: suppose that a buyer takes pity on a seller, and buys at a high price when he knows he could buy cheaper elsewhere; or suppose that a seller admires and respects the buyer and lets him buy cheap, when he knows he could have sold for more elsewhere. Has the market been corrupted? Is it working inefficiently? It depends on what you want the market to do. It is still being driven by supply and demand, but supply and demand are not here governed by financial considerations alone, any more than they are when a particular buyer prefers apples to oranges.

This leaves the third suggestion, that markets reward selfishness and greed, in that people do better in a market if they are selfish and greedy. But this certainly is not so. Basically, the market rewards the seller who provides the best product at the best price, and the buyer who buys it. They may be motivated by selfishness and greed but they do not have to be; and whatever motivates them, the market rewards them just the same. Perhaps his Lord came to him in the night and told him that what the world needs now is a roll-on under-arm deodorant, and Lo! what the world needed now was a roll-on under-arm deodorant, and he became very rich indeed. His motivation was not selfishness or greed or even self-interest, but piety and an obedience to the word of God. But so long as he provides the right product at the right price, the market will reward him. So far as the market is concerned, motivation is irrelevant.

At this point the argument may change track. The objection may become that even if markets do not reward selfishness and greed, neither do they penalize it, and that is a bad thing: people can be as selfish or greedy as they like and the market lets them get away with it. But this is not quite right either. The market can punish selfishness or greed just as it can reward other motivations. The point is that in bestowing its rewards, the market is indifferent to motivation of every sort: what matters is the bargains people strike, not why they strike them. This might, I suppose, be an objection of sorts, that the market seems not to care about selfishness or greed, or hope, or fear, or love, or enthusiasm, or the meaning of life itself. But if it is an objection, it is one which applies to much, much more than merely markets.

Competition

A second objection to the morality of markets is that markets encourage competition, and that that is a bad thing. This objection is much less diffuse than the previous one. It seems clear, first of all, that markets do not reward competition. On the contrary, markets reward co-operation: if sellers can get together, exclude all competitors, and drive the price up, they will do very well indeed; if buyers can get together, enforce a boycott, and drive the price down, they will do well too. Hence the need to keep the market open, if it is to work effectively. And for the same reason it also seems clear that the market ideology does not assume competition. It seems more plausible that people prefer the easy life, and that the point of keeping the market free and open if precisely to make life less easy than they might like. What does seem true, however, is that markets rely on competition for their efficient working, and in that sense they encourage, even demand, it. And that, so the argument goes, is a bad thing.

There is another important difference between this and the first objection. In the case of selfishness and greed it seems obvious enough that these are bad, but much less obvious that markets encourage them. In the case of competition it seems obvious enough that markets require it, but much less obvious that this is bad. So if we could only run the two arguments together, by arguing that competition encourages or requires selfishness and greed, we would have a single argument with the strengths of both and the weaknesses of neither.

One such argument would be that competition involves trying to do better than others, and that this involves ignoring, indeed over-riding, their interests, and especially their interest in doing better than you. If you were to take the interests of others in the competition into account, the competition would become a farce. Yet the pursuit of your own interests at the expense of the equally legitimate interests of others is precisely what is meant by selfishness. And selfishness is bad.

Thus one side in a game of football wants to score as many goals as possible, while preventing the other from scoring at all. The other side wants the same. If either side took the other's interests into account, and tried to further them at their own expense, the game would become a farce and no longer a competition (if they both tried it, it could become a different game, and a different competition). So in the interests of the competition, each side has to be selfish, pursuing its own interests at the expense of others. And not just selfish but greedy: if one team stops trying to score goals, because it has scored enough already, it has given up competing.

So the argument is that markets require competition; competition involves selfishness and greed, at least within the scope of the competition; but selfishness and greed are bad; so markets are bad too. Obviously, this argument proves too much. If it proves anything, it proves that not just markets but football, and tennis, and tiddly-winks are bad; and not just because they are competitive, as some have complained, but because they involve selfishness and greed, an accusation which seems even less plausible. This is because, in the context of a competition, and especially a competitive game, we do not call the pursuit of our own interests at the expense of others selfishness or greed. We speak of selfishness or greed only when this pursuit is bad or wrong or excessive; and since we do not think of it as bad or wrong or excessive within the context of a competitive game, we do not think of it as selfishness or greed.

If this is right it enables the defender of markets to turn the tables on his critic. Instead of having to accept both objections together, he can reject them together. Certainly markets encourage selfishness and greed, he may say. But in a competitive context, which is what a market is, we should not call them selfishness and greed. Transactions in the market are a sort of competitive game, like boxing, where normal moral considerations are suspended. Of course, people can hurt each other in a boxing ring, and take advantage of each other in a market. But there is nothing wrong with that; that is precisely what people go in to a boxing ring, or a market, to do. The participants expect nothing less, of themselves as well as each other.

This leaves us with the objection that competition is bad in itself, not because it involves selfishness and greed, but because of what it is. This

Don Locke

is the view that competition encourages rivalry and envy and promotes pride and arrogance in those who win, despair and a sense of worthlessness in those who lose. As against this there is the view that competition is an inevitable fact of life and an inescapable part of human nature, and the source and motivation of some of the human race's greatest achievements. There is much to say on either side, but these are large issues which have little to do with markets as such, and are more likely to obscure than clarify our present topic, so I will not pursue them further. There is, however, one point worth making.

One major source of competition, it will be argued, and one reason why it is futile to attempt to eliminate it, is scarcity. If there is enough of something for everyone, as was once the case with firewood, living space and unpolluted air, there will be no reason for people to compete for it. We can simply take what we want and know that there will be some left over for others. But if other things are in scarce supply, if there is not enough to go round, people will have to compete, one with another, to secure what they can. So long as there is scarcity, there will have to be competition. Moreover, the same is true of markets. If there is enough of some things for everyone, we do not need a market; we can simply take what we want. But if other things are in scarce supply, the market provides a mechanism for allocating them, in accordance with the laws of supply and demand. So, the argument goes, to object to the competitiveness of markets is to fail to understand why markets exist in the first place. Without competition for scarce resources you would not need a market; a market is simply a way of organizing competition for those resources which are in short supply.

This argument overstates the case, both for competition and for markets. Certainly the scarcity of resources is an inescapable fact of human life: not everyone can have everything they want; in all probability nobody can, not even the most hardened ascetic. But this sets us a problem, to which competition, via the market or in any other way, is only one possible solution. An alternative to the problem of scarcity is co-operation, or trying to find some fair and mutually-acceptable decision rule for the allocation of scarce resources. To each according to his needs, for example, not to each according to his ability to pay. This is the path that leads to a planned or controlled, not a free market, economy. I am not saying that this is necessarily a better solution to the problem. But I am saying that it is an alternative; competition and the market are not the only ways of allocating scarce resources.

Moreover the co-operative solution seems to accord more with morality as we normally understand it. Simplifying, we might say that there are two opposing approaches to any situation where the wishes or interests of some conflict with the wishes or interests of others. There is competition, where each party struggles to achieve their aims at the expense of the other; and there is co-operation, where we look for some independent and impartial resolution of the conflict. Morality, as we normally understand it, looks to the co-operative solution: we try to put ourselves in the position of others; we appeal to rules or principles which we would like to apply to ourselves and to others in similar situations; we look for solutions which can be regarded as universally binding, or at any rate universally applicable.

So to put it crudely, markets are about competition, morality is about co-operation. To that extent the market solution to the problem of scarce resources, is at odds with the moral solution. But it is a large jump from there to the conclusion that markets are positively immoral. For that we need more argument.

Character

A third moral criticism of markets is that the market ideology involves an attenuated and impoverished view of human nature. Human beings are seen as essentially, even solely, self-interested; or as abstract bearers of rights with no social connections, roles or commitments; or as nothing but owners of resources, including their own labour, for whom everything is a tradable commodity. This is the objection discussed in detail by Geoffrey Smith, so I will make only one comment here.

This is to enquire about the force of the objection. Once again it seems at first sight a factual, not a moral, point. Either these views about human nature are right or they are wrong. If they are wrong we can safely ignore them, except in so far as we feel an obligation to rescue others from their erroneous ideas. If they are right we had better believe them, even if we want to lament them. In neither case is it a moral criticism of the market. But here too this reply is too simple. When dealing with human psychology, believing something to be so can help to make it so. An impoverished view of human nature, if widely accepted and acted on, may help to impoverish us.

But how exactly does the market ideology produce or promote these conceptions of human nature? Is the objection that, without some such view of human character, you would not advocate the market as an efficient economic mechanism; and without its truth, markets would not in fact work effectively? This seems unlikely: the fact that some conceptualizations of the market are couched in dehumanizing terms does not mean that the market ideology positively requires them; on the contrary, the fact that some can support the market, at least in some situations, without endorsing those conceptions of human nature, suggests that they are extraneous additions, not essential ingredients. Instead the objection seems to be that some theorists are so impressed by the economic efficiency of markets that they speak as if human beings were nothing but traders in a market, as if an account of our roles and relationships in the market will suffice as an account of all human roles and relationships whatsoever. But if they do, this is a criticism of them, not of markets.

Autonomy

It is time we turned from the case against markets to the case in their favour. I said at the beginning of this paper that the major merit claimed for markets is that they are the most efficient mechanism known to us for providing people with what they want. This appears to be an economic merit; but is it perhaps a moral virtue as well?

For the Utilitarian, and especially the Preference Utilitarian (which, not wholly by accident, is what many economists are), giving people what they want, the satisfaction of their desires, is what morality is ultimately all about. But not everyone is a Preference Utilitarian. There is first the familiar problem of desire inflation, that as soon as you satisfy one desire, another desire arises, fully grown, to take its place. Paradoxically, the way to attain desire–satisfaction is not by satisfying your desires but by reducing them, to the level where you have only those desires which can be satisfied most easily. But more importantly, while markets may be the most efficient mechanism for ensuring that people get what they want, they may not be, indeed almost certainly are not, the most efficient mechanism for ensuring that people get what they need, or what they deserve. For that, a planned economy may be necessary after all. The present victory of market economics over planned economies may simply be the victory of desires over needs and merits.

Thus the economic merit of markets will be a moral virtue only if you rank desires above needs and deserts. But the justification will be that people's desires, and the strengths with which they have them, are the only valid measure of the value of goods and services. Needs and deserts are just desires which have got above their station. If I say I need or deserve something, I seem to be saying that I ought to be given what I desire; if I say that someone else needs or deserves something, I seem to be talking about what I want for them, whether or not they want it for themselves. If we seek to allocate goods or services by reference to peoples' needs or merits rather than their wants or desires, then we are in effect deciding for them how much they should have and of what.

In other words, the value ultimately at stake in this defence of markets is individual autonomy. The more you value the freedom to decide for yourself how you should live and what you should have, the more you will value the market, morally, as the best mechanism for ensuring that people do get what they have decided they want. I think, myself, that the virtue, as opposed to the value, of autonomy is over-rated. I agree that autonomy is a good thing and the more of it the better; but I do not believe that people can be assumed to have the ability to make the most sensible decisions on their own behalf. There are circumstances in which they have to be protected for themselves, and in their own interests. Autonomy, in so far as we have it, can be a mixed blessing.

Liberty and Equality

A second moral merit claimed for markets relies on the fact that for markets to work, if they are to be the most efficient mechanism for satisfying people's desires, they need to be both free and open: free in the sense that transactions are determined solely by the wishes and preferences of the transacting parties; and open in the sense that anyone can enter and trade on equal terms with anyone else. External inter-ference, in the form of government legislation, will distort the market, and ensure that it no longer delivers the goods in the most efficient manner. Closure, in the form of price-fixing cartels, will mean that the market no longer provides the best possible product at the best possible price.

The argument then is that these economic requirements are linked with political, and ultimately moral, values. Market freedom connects with political freedom, and market equality, meaning equality of access to the market, connects with political equality in the sense of equality of access to political power and decision making, in other words democ-racy. The argument is that each of these is impossible without the other, and the evidence seems to bear it out.

As against this, there is the argument that these two requirements of the market, that it be both free and open, cannot be satisfied together. The free market economy can be seen as a Darwinian struggle for existence where only the fittest survive. The effectiveness of the market is precisely that only those who deserve to survive, because they provide the best product at the best price, do survive. But eventually, when only the fittest have survived, they are in a position to impose their will on the market. As it has been put,[1] what starts in freedom ends in tyranny and bondage. But this will be true only so long as monopolies are also cartels, and are able to protect themselves from invasion of their markets by competitors who might undercut them. The problem,

---

[1] H. B. Acton, *The Morals Of Markets* (London: Longman, 1971), 9.

rather, is that the only way of keeping the market open may be to restrict its freedom, to have external interference in the form of anti-trust legislation.

This seems to me not a major difficulty. The defender of markets can say that the aim is, nevertheless, as much freedom and equality as possible, and that more is always better than less. The more important objection is that these virtues are a sham, that market freedom is not genuine freedom, and market equality not genuine equality.

Market freedom, first of all, is freedom from interference from others: it is a freedom to buy or sell without restriction or constraint from anybody, or any body. But this does not mean freedom from all restraints whatever. There are some things we may have to buy, and some times we may have to sell. If you are starving, for example, you may have to buy, or sell, whether you want to or not; it hardly matters, from your point of view, that it is not a person or an institution which makes you do it. Thus market freedom, by itself, is not enough. Even in a market, you are not really free if all you have is market freedom, freedom from interference from others. You need to be free in other ways as well, before you are really free to buy and sell as you please. It is not that real freedom needs market freedom; it is more that market freedom needs real freedom.

The same may also be true of political freedom. Political freedom is of course important and valuable. But how valuable is it if you are not free, for other reasons, to do the things it allows you to do? And it may even be that if we are to provide the more basic freedoms which make market and political freedom worth having, we have to interfere with market freedom, to ensure that those in need get more than the market itself would provide, and among other things ensure that they are put in a position where they can make effective use of whatever market freedom remains.

Similarly with market equality. Market equality is another form of freedom, the freedom to enter a market and trade on equal terms with anyone else. But how real is this equality, if there are other inequalities between us, before we even enter the market? To take the extreme example, if I am the only person on the island with a fresh water supply, in what sense are others free to enter the trade in water and compete with me on equal terms. Here too, we are not really equal, if all we have is market equality. It is not that real equality needs market equality; it is more that market equality needs real equality. Here too, the same may be true of political equality, in the sense of equality of access to political power. Political equality, like political freedom, is important and valuable. But how valuable is it, if some people are in a better position than others to make use of the advantages which political equality provides? And here too, it may be that if we are to provide the more basic equalities which make market and political equality worth having, we have to interfere with market equality, to ensure that the disadvantaged are put in a better position than the market itself would allow, and among other things ensure that they are in a position where they can make effective use of whatever market equality remains.

The Morals of the Market

The final argument I will consider is that so far from being in conflict with morality, markets actually require morals if they are to function properly, or function at all. Markets rely, and have to rely, on such virtues as honesty and trust and the keeping of agreements. This is not to say that people are always honest or reliable in markets, any more than they are always honest or reliable in other walks of life. But it is to say that the market makes virtues of them, which is what they ought to be.

The objection to this is liable to be that if this is morality, it is a very limited one. The virtues it acknowledges are few, and they are acknowledged only because they are necessary to the workings of markets, not because they are valuable, or moral, in themselves. The point is nicely illustrated by Acton, in the course of arguing against the claim that markets are essentially amoral or immoral:

> it is obvious that moral conduct, in the sense of conduct that is morally right or wrong and is in general subject to moral standards, does take place in the market . . . For in the market people can be just or unjust, honest or dishonest, reliable or unreliable, and these are moral characteristics. They can also be cautious or rash, and these may be regarded as moral characteristics too . . .
>
> On examination, therefore, we find that there is absolutely nothing in the complaint that markets are by their very nature immoral or amoral, although many of those participate in them cheat or would cheat if they dared. All that remains to charge the market with on this score . . . is that in it the Christian virtues of humility, charity and self-sacrifice are not displayed . . .
>
> But how could humility, charity and self-sacrifice be shown in the market? If we ask how they could be exercised by business firms, the absurdity of the question becomes apparent . . . The very idea of a firm showing humility or sacrificing itself is absurd, and the idea of these virtues being exercised by individual participants in the market is hardly less so.[2]

[2] *The Morals of Markets,* 19–20.

Unfortunately, these things are absurd only in the sense that we cannot imagine them happening, not in the sense that they are inconceivable. It is perfectly possible for an individual in a market situation, and even a business, to show humility or self-sacrifice, to insist that their product may not be as good as people think it is, or to close the operation down because the product is dangerous. But it is hard to believe that it would ever happen.

What this suggests is that the morals you find in markets will be limited to those virtues which enable markets to work well. As the quotation seems to show, there will be little scope for those virtues which actually work against the workings of markets, and especially for the Christian virtues, in the sense of virtues associated with the name of Christ.

Finally

I cannot myself see much morality in markets, nor can I see them as working to the moral, as opposed to economic, good of the human race. But neither can I see them as essentially immoral, as working against morality, or as a positive force for evil. If I were to evaluate markets myself I would look not to their economic merits, or to their moral virtues and vices, but to their social effects. But that, luckily, would have to be another paper.

Liberal Man

SUSAN MENDUS

I begin with two quotations: one from Anthony Crosland's *Socialism Now*, the other from Thucydides' account of the Peloponnesian War. Crosland says:

> experience shows that only a small minority of the population wish to participate [in politics]. I repeat what I have often said—the majority prefer to lead a full family life and cultivate their gardens. And a good thing too . . . we do not necessarily want a busy, bustling society in which everyone is politically active and fussing around in an interfering and responsible manner, and herding us all into participating groups. *The threat to privacy and freedom would be intolerable*.[1]

This is the voice of twentieth-century liberal man—of a man whose values are the values of individual privacy and freedom. By contrast, Thucydides says (or, more accurately, reports Pericles as saying):

> Here [in the polis] each individual is interested not only in his own affairs but in the affairs of state as well . . . we do not say that a man who takes no interest in politics is a man who minds his own business: we say that he has no business here at all.[2]

The two quotations highlight the different roles played by privacy and community in twentieth-century liberal society and the Athenian polis respectively. Whereas in liberal society, the public or political sphere is a more or less necessary evil, secondary to the home, the family and private life, for the Athenians the situation was almost the reverse. As Crosland notes, the central values now are values of privacy and individual freedom, and the state exists to protect privacy and individual freedom. The state, in other words, is subordinate to individuals. In fifth century Athens, by contrast, the central values were the values of community, friendship, and citizenship, and the individual was fulfilled when he pursued those communal ends. Put crudely, the state

---

[1] Anthony Crosland, *Socialism Now* (London: Cape, 1974), 89. As quoted in A. Arblaster, *The Rise and Decline of Western Liberalism* (Oxford: Blackwell, 1984), 44; my emphasis.
[2] Thucydides, *The Peloponnesian War*, as quoted in Arblaster, *Western Liberalism*.

did not exist to serve the individual; the individual existed as part of the state.

Here, then, is one characteristic of liberal man: liberal man is a private and retiring man. He cultivates his garden, protects his privacy, minds his own business, keeps himself largely to himself. His loyalties are to his family and friends, not to the state. He is a man to whom the notion of community, in any strong sense, is alien.

A second characteristic of liberal man may be identified via two further quotations: one from a recent speech by the Conservative politician, John Moore, the other from the ancient Greek poet, Pindar. Justifying government changes in the National Health Service Moore, says;

> a climate of dependence can in time corrupt the human spirit. Everyone knows the sullen apathy of dependence and can compare it with the sheer delight of personal achievement. To deliberately set up a system that creates the former instead of the latter is to act directly against the best interests and indeed the welfare of individuals and of society. The job therefore has been to change this depressing climate of dependence and revitalize the belief which has been such a powerful force throughout British history: that individuals *can* take action to change their lives; *can* do things to control what happens to them. We believe that dependence in the long run decreases human happiness and reduces human freedom. We believe that the well being of individuals is best protected and promoted when they are helped to be independent, to use their talents to take care of themselves, and to achieve things on their own which is one of the greatest satisfactions life can offer.[3]

Twentieth-century liberal man aspires to make his own life, control his own fate, and triumph over the contingencies of background, circumstance, and environment. By contrast, Pindar adopts a more accepting and (some would say) submissive attitude. He writes;

> But human excellence
> grows like a vine tree,
> fed by the green dew,
> raised up among wise men and just
> to the liquid sky.
> We have all kinds of needs for those we love
> most of all in hardships, but joy, too,
> strains to track down eyes that it can trust.[4]

[3] John Moore, Conservative Political Centre publication, October 1987.

[4] Pindar *Nemean*, VIII. 37–44, as quoted in Martha C. Nussbaum, *The Fragility of Goodness* (Cambridge University Press, 1986), vi.

Here the emphasis is (both literally and metaphorically) on roots: man is not a controlling creature, striving to triumph over circumstance, but a dependent and needy creature, sunk in the contingencies of fate and chance. Like the vine tree, his well-being is dictated by things over which he has little or no control—sunlight, water, the green dew and the liquid sky. Moreover, and most importantly, this is not a source of regret, for human flourishing in Pindar's eyes is not *opposed* to dependence, it is defined in terms of dependence. As Martha Nussbaum has put it; 'human excellence is seen in Pindar's poem, and pervasively in the Greek poetic tradition, as something whose very nature it is to be in need, a growing thing that could not be made invulnerable and keep its own peculiar fineness'.[5] Again, there is a gulf between the twentieth-century liberal view and the Greek view: where liberal man aspires to create his own life and to control the world, the Greek character accepts his dependent status, his vulnerability as a *part of* the world.

The two sets of quotations provide the themes of this paper: liberal man is private and solitary (he is a free and independent self), whereas Greek man is essentially a member of a community (he is defined by his role in society). Liberal man is autonomous and controlling (he *chooses* the commitments which constitute the self—commitments to his wife, his friends, his children), whereas Greek man is dependent and determined (he *accepts* his role within the world—acknowledges obligations which are largely unchosen—obligations to siblings, parents, the city state). So, where liberalism extols the value of autonomy, Pindar extols the value of dependence. Where liberalism extols the value of privacy, Thucydides (Pericles) extols the value of community. Put generally, where liberalism extols the value of the *chosen*, the Greek world extols the value of the *given*.

My aim in this paper is to discuss the implications of these different views of human nature and human fulfilment. In particular, I shall discuss the liberal commitment to independence—to achieving things on one's own. My claims will be that in so far as this purports to present a picture of what life is like, it is false; in so far as it purports to present a picture of what life ought to be like, it is morally impoverished, and in so far as it aspires to explain the human condition it is partial and distorting. We are more like the vine tree than liberals would have us believe, and there is reason to be grateful that that is so. In general, then, I shall be arguing for the practical and moral necessity of a move away from the liberal language of choice and towards the language of dependence.

[5] Op. cit., 2.

Susan Mendus

In pursuing my aim I shall follow two distinct but connected paths: firstly, I shall consider a twentieth-century literary example, the example of George and Lennie in John Steinbeck's novel, *Of Mice and Men*. My aim here is to indicate that the model of man as independent and controlling is false to the realities of all our lives. Moreover, there is an important sense in which we should not aspire to this ideal: achieving things on our own, far from being the greatest satisfaction life can offer, is an aspiration which often turns out to be hollow.

Secondly, I shall consider the example of Antigone in Sophocles' play of that name. My aim here is to suggest that the whole nature of tragic circumstances is distorted by the liberal perspective. Liberal emphasis on man as a free and independent chooser not only misrepresents the realities of our lives, it also renders tragic circumstances incomprehensible. So the Steinbeck case enables us to see how the liberal conception of man as independent and controlling is an unwarranted idealization (it presents a distorted picture of what human flourishing consists in); the Antigone case enables us to see how the liberal conception of man as a free and independent self is an unacceptable abstraction (it cannot accommodate central features of our lives).

Steinbeck and Human Dependence

I turn first, then, to Steinbeck's *Of Mice and Men* and to a discussion of human dependence. Steinbeck's novel tells of two characters—George and Lennie. George and Lennie are migrant labourers who roam the Salinas Valley, moving from ranch to ranch in constant search of work. Together, they make an incongruous pair: George is small, shrewd, alert; Lennie a cretinous giant, barely able to think or remember the simplest things. His massive strength leads him to destroy the objects of his affection, and George is his guardian, saving him from the worst consequences of his own idiocy. George aspires to be the independent man. His constant refrain is of how good it would be if he were able to control his own life, to achieve things on his own. 'God a'mighty,' he says,

> if I was alone I could live so easy. I could go get a job an' work, an' no trouble. No mess at all, and when the end of the month come I could take my fifty bucks and go into town and get whatever I want. Why, I could stay in a cat house all night. I could eat anyplace I want, hotel or any place, and order any damn thing I could think of. An' I could do that every damn month.[6]

This is George's dream, the dream of discovering 'one of the greatest satisfactions life can offer', the dream of independence. But there is

[6] John Steinbeck, *Of Mice and Men*, (Reading: Pan, 1974) 15.

another dream too, a dream which he shares with Lennie. They speak of it by the river as the novel begins, and again at its pathetic conclusion.

> 'Someday—we're gonna get the jack together and gonna have a little house and a couple of acres an' a cow and some pigs and—' 'An' live off the fatta the lan' Lennie shouted. 'An' have rabbits. Go on George! Tell about what we're gonna have in the garden and about the rabbits in the cages and about the rain in the winter and the stove, and how thick the cream is on the milk, like you can hardly cut it. Tell about that, George . . .'[7]

This second dream is their 'best laid scheme', their 'promis'd joy'. It comes to nothing. Once again Lennie kills the thing he loves—their new employer's daughter—and George is forced to shoot him to keep him from being lynched. The story displays, in graphic detail, the extent to which the two protagonists are dependent creatures. In particular, their dependency consists in their vulnerability to three distinct forms of luck—constitutional luck (luck in their character) circumstantial luck (luck in their world); and consequential luck (luck in the way things turn out for them). These forms of luck make them victims of the world, rather than controllers of it. Lennie, in particular, is a victim: of his character, which makes him kill the things he loves; of his circumstances, which force him to move from place to place looking for work; and of consequences, since his good will delivers disastrous outcomes quite the reverse of his intentions. Moreover, and most importantly, in Steinbeck's vision 'Lennie was to be, not a pathetic cretin, but a symbolic figure . . . a Lennie who was not to represent insanity at all, but the inarticulate and powerful yearnings of all men.' Lennie's best laid scheme is doomed to failure, but it is doomed not because he is Lennie the imbecilic giant, but because he is human. His fate is (potentially) the fate of us all in so far as we are vulnerable to things outside our control.

The story directs attention to a form of dependence which involves absence of control. It suggests that we cannot always, or with any degree of certainty, 'take action to change our lives', nor can we 'do things to control what happens to us'. Much of the pathos of the story lies in the very fact that George and Lennie are victims of the world in which they find themselves. And much of its power lies in the implication that the rest of us are, at root, no different from them. We are none of us in control of our 'best laid schemes'. But the story also draws attention to another form of dependence, which connects control and neediness. In the poem from Pindar this kind of dependence is also

[7] Ibid., 18. See also 93.

referred to: Pindar sees human beings as both vulnerable (subject to things outside their control) and needy. By contrast liberals characteristically assume not only that we *can* control our lives (that we are to some degree invulnerable), but also that we will flourish better if we *do* control our lives (that we are, to some degree, not in need of things external to us). Thus John Moore speaks of individuals' ability to 'achieve things *on their own*', which is, he says, 'one of the greatest satisfactions life can offer'. Similarly, John Stuart Mill speaks enthusiastically of the man who is active, energetic, controlling. 'It is', he says, 'the privilege *and proper condition* of a human being arrived at the maturity of his faculties, to use and interpret experience in his own way, to decide what part of recorded experience is properly applicable to his own circumstances and character.'[8] Men should, in Mill's view 'choose their own plan of life', mould and fashion their own world. They should employ judgment, choice, discrimination. In general, Mill's vision is the vision of man as a controlling creature—one who does not allow others or the world to determine his plan of life, but who achieves things on his own. The first lesson of Steinbeck's novel is that this is not always possible: like George and Lennie we may be dependent on circumstances and on character in a way which will make independent achievement impossible.

But a second lesson of Steinbeck's novel is that such achievement will not necessarily satisfy. When George is forced to shoot Lennie, he does not discover the benefits of independence, but rather its hollowness. He discovers that his personal dream—his dream of freedom and self-determination—is in fact empty. 'George is left with the free life he claimed to want, but which he actually dreaded, recognizing, though never admitting, its utter futility and loneliness.' Independence (the ability to achieve things on his own) far from being one of the greatest satisfactions life can offer, destroys the possibility of satisfaction. Despite George's professed aspiration to independence, he is highly dependent on Lennie. It is this dependence which gives meaning to his life and which makes him a proper object of our admiration.

Here, then, are two ways in which we may understand dependence: as vulnerability, or susceptibility to luck, which determines how well or ill our plans go; and as neediness, or dependence on others for our own well-being, which determines what value our plans have for us. I have sugested that in the former case dependence is an ineradicable feature of human life, and that in the latter case dependence can be the thing which makes our plans and our lives meaningful. So at one and the same time we are dependent because we cannot control our 'best-laid schemes', and dependent because those schemes make essential refer-

[8] J. S. Mill, *On Liberty* (Harmondsworth: Penguin, 1978), 122.

ence to others for their significance and value. Put together, these two forms of dependence cast doubt both upon the claim that we can control our lives and upon the claim that such control is 'one of the greatest satisfactions life can offer'. They undermine the liberal idealization of independence as a way of life.

Before discussing the implications of these examples, I want to draw one further contrast between conceptions of human nature as dependent, and conceptions of human nature as controlling. Steinbeck's major novels, written in the late 1930s and early 1940s, make constant reference to the coming of the machine, and to the ways in which the machine destroys the American Dream of endeavour rewarded. *The Grapes of Wrath* is, of course, the most obvious place where antagonism between man and machine is discussed. The Joads of Oklahoma are the victims of a burgeoning technology which denies them their birthright of a chicken in every pot and a car in every garage. As 'man' becomes more powerful over nature, individual men become impotent, or they become 'machine men'. Steinbeck speaks of 'the machine man, driving a dead tractor on land he does not know and love, [he] understands only chemistry; and he is contemptuous of the land and of himself. When the corrugated iron doors are shut, he goes home, and his home is not the land'.[9]

The pursuit of technological supremacy—of control over nature—makes man less human. The analogy now is not between man and things in nature, like the vine tree. Rather the analogy is between man and the things which tame nature—the tractor, the machinery of the new technology. Man is no longer a part of the natural world, but a being distinct from the natural world, who manipulates it for his own purposes. And in this, Steinbeck implies, there is a loss of something characteristically human, for men do not simply use the machinery of the new world, they become like machines themselves. In the pursuit of technological omnipotence man becomes more like a tool himself. His value is no longer an intrinsic value, defined by reference to his neediness, but an instrumental value, defined in terms of the power he can exert over other things.

In his *Groundwork for a Metaphysic of Morals* Kant tells us that everything in the world has either a price or a dignity. As we cease to see human beings as akin to things in the natural world (the vine tree), and construe them as akin to machines, we abandon dignity in favour of price: we lose a sense of distinctively human value, and reduce everything to instrumental value, forgetting that where everything has instrumental value, nothing has dignity at all.

[9] John Steinbeck, *The Grapes of Wrath* (Pan, Suffolk, 1975), 124.

Of Mice and Men thus indicates two ways in which human beings are dependent: we are vulnerable to luck, and we are needy. We cannot eradicate the former kind of dependence, and we should not seek to eradicate the latter. The former puts success and failure at least partly beyond our control. This is not necessarily a source of regret. Our dependence on other people is what gives value to the success of our projects. Without it, we might succeed in controlling our own lives, but the victory would be a hollow and empty one. The reason for this is given in the final example—the example from *The Grapes of Wrath*: Steinbeck's notorious 'earthiness' suggests that it is not dependence in itself which is either good or bad. Rather, value springs from what we are dependent on. There are forms of dependence which assert our value as human beings, and there are forms of dependence which deny it. The dependence which implies that, as human beings, we have only an instrumental value is the worst form of dependence. It is this which is implied in the move from an analogy between man and the natural world to an analogy between man and the inanimate objects of the new technology. It is the very rejection of dependency (the neediness and vulnerability of the vine tree) which brings with it the denial of humanity.

Sophocles and the Nature of Tragedy

The example of George and Lennie illustrates the extent to which liberal emphasis on control and independence presents a distorted picture of human life. It is false to the facts of our lives and false also to our values, for we are not merely and as a matter of fact vulnerable and dependent. It is also the case that dependence is often the thing which invests our lives with meaning. Our frailty is, in this respect, also part of our fineness.

This last thought draws attention to the sense in which the liberal conception of agency may be an idealization, rather than a mere abstraction. Liberals often employ the notion of independence to refer to the kind of people we should aspire to be. Thus, John Moore advocates achieving things on one's own (this is not only what we do do, but what we should do), Mill speaks of the importance of choosing one's own style of life ('the privilege and *proper condition* of a human being'), and similarly John Rawls appeals to 'an ideal' of persons as independent and autonomous. Writing about Rawls, Onora O'Neill says:

A *Theory of Justice* was tailored to hide the interlocking structure of desires and attitudes that is typical of human agents. Once the social relations between agents were masked it could seem plausible to . . . build a determinate ideal of mutual independence into a conception of justice. This ideal is not met by any human agents. It isn't only deficient and backward human agents whose choosing would be misrepresented by these ideal agents of construction. The construction assumes a mutual independence which is false of all human beings. Such independence is as much an idealization of human social relations as an assumption of generalized altruism would be.[10]

The Steinbeck story may be read as an attempt to express precisely this: that liberalism assumes a mutual independence which is in fact not ours. In so doing it idealizes a picture of man as an independent chooser, but man is not an independent chooser. Man exists within complex networks of dependency, many of which are nothing to do with choice at all.

All this, however, is an attack on the idealization of independence, but characteristically liberals deny that they are idealizing at all. Rather, they claim merely to be simplifying by removing the contingencies which clutter everyday life. The earlier references to Mill and Rawls cast doubt on whether this is really true, but even if it were true, a problem persists, which is to establish the criteria whereby some things are deemed to be contingent and others are not. How, in other words, can we know how much to abstract? It is here that the cultural specificity of liberal thinking becomes clear. For even if the liberal conception of human agents as mutually independent is 'our' conception, it is not thereby a universal conception, and this fact can lead to a distortion of our understanding of other ways of thinking. Put simply, the form of my argument is this: either liberal appeal to independence is an idealization or it is an abstraction. If it is an idealization, it is one which is false to our lives. We are victims as often as we are choosers. If, on the other hand, it is an abstraction, what warrants the decision to cull *this* from the process of abstraction, rather than something else? Who says that when we have abstracted we will be left with man as an independent chooser and controller, rather than man as merely one needy thing amongst others? My second example is an attempt to grapple with this problem.

Sophocles' *Antigone* tells of the tragic choice which faces Antigone when the laws of the state and the laws of the gods conflict. Her brother, Polynices, has died a traitor's death attacking his own city. As dictated by convention, Creon, the ruler, declares that his body is to be left unburied. But Antigone cannot comply. Disobeying the laws of the state, she buries Polynices and her punishment is death.

Antigone is one of the most comprehensively studied of Sophocles' plays, and a major debate amongst commentators is whether the character of Antigone represents moral right and Creon moral wrong,

[10] Onora O'Neill, 'Contructivisms in Ethics', *Proceedings of the Aristotelian Society*, LXXXIX (1989/9), 5.

or whether there is a sense in which both are wrong. Does Antigone have too narrow a vision of moral duty, or is she the true representation of moral innocence, uncorrupted by political considerations of power and control? There is a sense in which the terms of that debate are themselves suffused with the liberal vision of man (in this case woman) as an active chooser. It is far less clear that the question arises in quite that way from outside the liberal tradition—from the Greek perspective itself. Why is this so?

Three thoughts are relevant here: firstly, that the tragic nature of Antigone's situation is evident only if we assume (as liberalism does not) that individuals are not merely selves, but also the occupiers of roles. Secondly, that the very nature of tragedy presupposes a non-liberal conception of human nature as dependent, not controlling. Thirdly, that the concept of community plays a central role in generating and explaining the tragedy. These three themes are evident in the commentaries on *Antigone* presented by three modern philosophers: Martin Hollis, Martha Nussbaum, and Alasdair MacIntyre. I shall conclude by discussing these briefly.

Hollis adopts a characteristically liberal approach to the tragedy. He claims that, whilst Antigone and Creon are both '*dramatis personae* in the old sense of "masks" or complete embodiments of role. Yet they both *choose* their doomed paths . . . this need not imply', he says, 'that other choices would have saved them, but it does imply that Sophocles is thinking in terms of individual agency.'[11] This seems to me to be a misrepresentation of the situation: of course, in so far as Antigone does something (rather than nothing), it is appropriate to say that she chooses. But the whole force of the tragedy is to indicate that the choices she makes are not choices *qua* individual agent, but choices *qua* occupier of a role. The liberal conception of individual agency (of a self) is largely inappropriate here, for there is nothing in Antigone, as an individual agent, which is relevant to the tragedy. The whole genesis of the tragic situation is directly attributable to the seriousness with which she accepts her role.

Thus, for example, the play begins with the cry 'O sister!' and Antigone goes on immediately to describe 'the death of our two brothers', and how she and Ismene are doomed to suffer 'for our father'. It is the fact that she is circumscribed by these societal roles which determines Antigone's fate. She does not choose in the way the liberal man would choose—as an independent self; she 'chooses' as a sister. More properly, she accepts the duties which the role of sister impose her, and reminds Ismene that Polynices is their brother, 'whether we

[11] Martin Hollis, *The Cunning of Reason* (Cambridge University Press, 1987), 208.

like it or not'. In brief, her situation is not one of an individual agent who decides, but of a sister who acknowledges and accepts. This, then, is one aspect of the tragedy of Antigone: it is central to the play that she does not act as a free and independent liberal self.

A second feature, emphasized by Alasdair MacIntyre, is the relationship between tragedy and value pluralism. It is a commonplace in modern political philosophy that liberals are commited to a plurality of goods, some of which conflict with others. The guiding vision of liberalism is the vision of society as an association of independent agents who have distinct and sometimes incompatible conceptions of the good. Liberal societies do not attempt to impose their conception of the good on their citizens, rather they provide a neutral arena within which the agents themselves may decide upon and pursue their own conception of the good. Thus, the liberal scheme of things assumes a plurality of values. In general, what legitimates the choice of values is just that—that it is a choice.

By contrast, MacIntyre urges that Sophocles' claim is *both* that goods are irreconcilable (there is a plurality of values) *and* that there is an objective moral order. The tragic heroine is not, like the liberal, simply confronted by a bewildering array of choices, some of which conflict with others. She is also haunted by the knowledge that there is a right choice. 'There are indeed crucial conflicts in which different virtues appear as making different and incompatible claims upon us. But our situation is tragic in that we have to recognize the authority of both claims'.[12] Here is the locus of at least some liberal misunderstanding of tragedy. Ackerman, for example, argues that 'there are no moral meanings hidden in the bowels of the universe. There is only you and I struggling in a world which neither we nor any other thing created'.[13] This certainly makes life difficult, but it cannot, I think, make life tragic. The problem for the liberal is to establish which is the rational choice amongst the many conflicting values. But the problem for the tragic hero is to know, to acknowledge, what is right. He cannot escape his predicament by choosing, because more than choice is required. Knowledge is required. And knowledge is precisely what he cannot have.

Finally, and connectedly, both Alasdair MacIntyre and Martha Nussbaum emphasize the central role of community in the Greek conception. Whereas, for us, the role of friendship, company, and city state are contingent, in the Greek conception they are central. The entire ethical experience of tragedy, says Nussbaum, 'stresses the fun-

[12] Alasdair MacIntyre, *After Virtue* (London: Duckworth, 1981), 134.
[13] B. A. Ackerman *Social Justice in the Liberal State*, Yale University Press, 1980, 368.

damental value of community and friendship. It does not invite or even permit us to seek for the good apart from these'.[14] In so far, therefore, as modern liberal thinking abstracts from the values of friendship and community, it abstracts what may well be contingent in our lives, but is essential to the Greek tragedians. Moreover, the point can be generalized beyond the considerations thrown up by *Antigone*: Rawls' *Theory of Justice* offers a coherent articulation of the deep moral commitments of 'our' society. We are invited to read the book as a vindication of the principles of justice 'we' would discover in drawing on 'our' underlying conceptions of free and equal citizenship. But as has been pointed out, 'this vindication of justice does not address others who, unlike "us", do not start with such ideals of citizenship; it has nothing to say to those others'.[15]

These three themes express three reservations about the role of abstraction in liberal theory: a reservation about how we can know what we should abstract; a reservation about what we are left with after we have abstracted (are we left with an agent who is a chooser, or a tragic character who acknowledges fate?), and a reservation about what, if anything, we can say to the inhabitant of a different culture whose process of abstraction proceeds differently.

Conclusion

I began by mentioning two features characteristic of liberal man: he is a private self rather than the occupier of a social role; and he is an independent agent, who aspires to control his world. Put together, these features generate a conception of human agents as essentially choosing and deciding, rather than accepting or acknowledging. This conception was then contrasted with an alternative conception implicit in some of the literature of ancient Greece. The point of the contrast, and of the subsequent examples, was two-fold: firstly to draw a distinction between independence as an abstraction and independence as an idealization. Secondly to suggest that neither of these is adequate. The Steinbeck example aims to show that in so far as independence is an ideal, it is not an ideal to which we either do or should subscribe. There are many circumstances in which dependence is both an ineradicable fact of life, and also something which gives value to our plans and projects. We are not essentially independent and controlling creatures, and we have reason to be glad that that is so.

By contrast, the Antigone example aims to show that in so far as independence is an abstraction, it is one which misrepresents the nature

---

[14] Nussbaum, *The Fragility of Goodness*, 70.
[15] O'Neill, Constructivisms in Ethics', 8.

of some, tragic, circumstances, The decision to abstract from an agent's role as sister, mother, father, subject within the state, is a decision to assert liberal values. It is not a justification of those values.

Moreover, in abstracting, we run the risk of failing to see the truly tragic nature of some situations. Antigone's tragedy lies not in the fact that she is faced with a choice between competing values, but in the fact that she must be dishonoured. The liberal conception of man as agent—as independent free chooser—leaves room for difficult choices, even impossible choices. But it does not leave room for tragic *situations* . Commenting on this, one philosopher has written;

> Consider what might happen in a society where, increasingly, the limitations of character and the situations which limit moral endeavour are not recognized. It is probable that the idea that there must be a solution to every difficulty would become even more prevalent than it is already in certain circles today. If this were to happen, the very idea of what a difficulty is would have changed in important respects. Difficulties would be regarded as signs that something had gone wrong, in much the same way as a flaw in a product shows that there is something wrong in the techniques of production.[16]

At the limit, the language of independence and control leaves no room for the tragic or the pathetic. The thoughts that life was too hard, that fortune was fickle, that burdens were too great cannot sensibly be accommodated by this way of looking at the world. Independence and control require effort, not acceptance. They allow only bad judgments, faulty calculations, incomplete equations. Tragedy, however, works in quite the opposite way, directing our attention to cases where trying is precisely not what is required. To the extent that this is so, the language of liberal individualism, the language of control and independence robs us of the means to understand others, and it may also rob us of an understanding of an important part of ourselves.

[16] D. Z. Phillips 'Some Limits to Moral Endeavour', in *Through a Darkening Glass*, (Oxford: Blackwell, 1982), 47–8.

Liberal Man
A Response

PETER BINNS

Liberalism and politics

One philosopher recently claimed that liberalism's distinguishing feature 'is that liberal social proposals are more permissive and accommodating to variety'.[1] He may well have been right about the way the term is used in common speech, where 'liberal' and 'soft' are sometimes used synonymously, but I think that following this path is particularly unfruitful in the philosophical illumination of *politics*. 'Permissive' and 'accommodating' social proposals are, after all, to be found in a wide spectrum of opinion from far right to far left, and it is not at all the case that any move to the liberal centre must always be expected to involve a move towards such 'accommodating' policies.

Sometimes indeed it is quite the reverse. When Brazil's right-wing generals handed over power to a constitutional centre party, the move was applauded by *The Economist* which believed that it would lead to less 'permissive' social policies and therefore to more money being available to repay the international banks. But surely it only adds confusion to try to fit this move into a schema which defines it as a move from the *liberalism* of a right-wing dictatorship to the *illiberalism* of what followed, as the above definition would have us do?

But even if we exclude the non-political theories of liberalism that seek to define it in terms such as 'softness' versus 'hardness', we are still left with a problem. For, at some times and in some places, the welfare state, backed up by the theories of one liberal, John Maynard Keynes, is seen as the centrepiece of liberal social policy, while more recently Margaret Thatcher is seen as dismantling it in the name of another set of liberal theories, those associated with the liberal individualism of Friedman, Hayek and the Austrian school.

So even if we confine ourselves to political liberalism, the terrain seems excessively wide. At first sight it is indeed difficult to see what it is that Keynesianism, with its commitment to state intervention in the economy, and the theorists of the New Right, with their commitment to end it, could possibly have in common. The Keynesian picture

[1] N. Dent, 'The "tensions" of Liberalism', *Philosophical Quarterly* (October 1988), 484.

seems to suggest that there is an ineradicable dimension of collective life within which the state must act if the life of its citizens is to be acceptable. The state therefore has a perfect right to impose taxes even on those individuals who do not consent to them, and a duty to take upon itself the decision as to what proportion of the national product should be allocated for individual consumption and what proportion should be allocated for collective consumption. Is it not precisely the contrast between this 'collectivist consensus' of earlier post-war British governments and the line taken by the present government that has required the coining of a new term, 'Thatcherism'? How can there be important similarities between these views when one is faced with such fundamental dissimilarities, one between collectivism and individualism?

But this line of thinking has unfortunate consequences. It makes it seem that while Thatcher and Keynes would make bad bedfellows as economic policymakers, Stalin and Keynes—both 'collectivists' by this definition—would not. What this ignores is the purpose and intention behind economic policymaking and the different historical circumstances in which it takes place. John Maynard Keynes, writing in the midst of an economic crisis in which the world's economies had retreated into largely autonomous zones—the Sterling zone in the Empire, the dollar zone, the yen co-prosperity zone in Asia etc.—could perceive recovery in terms of demand management by the state at the centre of each zone using its fiscal power as a central instrument of economic and political policy. The problems facing Thatcher in 1979 were the other way about. The creation of a global capital market had undermined the interventionist state and all its fiscal tools (as Callaghan had already discovered in the two years prior to Thatcher's succession). On the other hand the world economy—unlike in the 1930s—was still growing, so the Keynesian solution seemed neither possible nor necessary in the 1980s.

One might be inclined to conclude from this that even 'political liberalism' is a hopelessly ambiguous term which conflates such entirely distinct concepts as 'unconstrained laissez-faire' and 'welfarism'; but this would be a mistake. A more fruitful approach is to look at the theories of man which seem to underly liberalisms and see what common ground can be found there. Is there is unifying concept of the person that they presuppose, and if so what is there to be said about it, and what can it most usefully be compared and contrasted with?

Liberal man

Thatcher and Keynes, for all their differences, did not have two *philosophically opposed* theories of what human beings are or should be.

On the contrary, they both sought to defend, in very different historical circumstances, the continuance of the laissez-faire economy as far as it seemed possible, and, with it, the sort of individuals who are created by—and thrive within—this economy. To get the market going, to be sure, will involve certain constraints and some costs in terms of the background social, political and economic infrastructural inputs needed, and there can be differences of opinion as well as differences of historical circumstances here, but these have to be seen in terms of the common aim to create the best possible circumstances for the flourishing of the laissez-faire economy and the *autonomous individuals whose joint activity constitute this economy*.

What these conceptions have in common—and how they differ from certain other conceptions of political man—was clarified by Sir Isaiah Berlin twenty-five years ago.[2] According to this view liberalism is defined in accordance with its conception of autonomy or liberty, which is seen purely *negatively* as a lack of constraints on individuals. This is contrasted with the *positive* conception of liberty to be found, for instance, in anti-liberal thinkers like Hegel, where liberty consists in the ability to participate in the on-going process of the development of society. What is important about Berlin's notion is that it puts the conception of human beings at the centre of the analysis, and in doing so it renders the question of the best kind of economic and political structure to fit such human beings into being a secondary one. What makes both Thatcher and Keynes into liberals on this conception is therefore their common belief that the role of social policy—whatever that policy might be—is to optimize the negative liberty available to autonomous individuals within society.

Susan Mendus, in her paper, develops a critique of liberalism, that is also focused on the conception of human nature that it contains. She argues that liberalism ignores the 'vulnerability' and 'neediness' of human beings. These features are not imperfections, but part of our essence: we cannot remove our vulnerability while keeping our own peculiar fineness and in doing so becoming less human. To adopt a one-sided view of human beings as simply controlling and self-determining is impoverishing. Experiencing and learning about the boundaries to our power (through, for instance, the literature of tragedy) is essential for a fully-rounded account of what makes us into real people, and to do that we therefore need to go beyond liberalism. If self-sufficient autonomy were simply to be maximized, this would remove our vulnerability, and, along with it, our humanity and our particular excellence as human beings.

[2] *Four Essays on Liberty* (Oxford University Press, 1969).

This view has important implications. It would seem to be directed not just against liberalism, but also against some theories which sharply contrast with it in other ways, like Marxism for instance, which is also committed to emphasizing the self-determining dimension of human nature. In fact all theorists who put human *power* at the centre of their account of human nature would seem to be logically implicated in Susan Mendus's attack. Her critique provides some of the reasons why liberal individualism has seemed incapable of depicting the relationship between the self and the cosmos in anything other than alien and antagonistic terms. And, as a result, it also might seem to provide a useful framework for expressing at least some kinds of ecological concern that might otherwise get neglected.

However, in this paper I would like to argue for two things with respect to this thesis; firstly I would like to explore the sorts of strategems that liberals might adopt in replying, and secondly I would like to develop the view that the notions of 'neediness' and vulnerability' have other—and more damaging—consequences for liberalism if looked at more closely. Above all they raise serious questions about the viability of the account of the individual which both the liberal and Susan Mendus—if only implicitly—offer us.

One liberal response: primary and secondary conceptions of the self

What sort of response might a liberal give to such a criticism? One 'muscular' rejoinder might simply be to dismiss this vulnerable and needy side of ourselves altogether as simply an atavistic hangover from a bygone world that is now, thankfully, in the past. Most liberals, however, do seem to recognize that it represents a crucial and ineradicable dimension of our nature. How might they answer the charge that it seems incompatible with the very idea of liberal man?

Firstly they may argue—as Margaret Thatcher has argued after her 1987 election victory—that traditional community values are needed to *supplement* the autonomous individualism that is to be encouraged in the market place. On this view the market, and the mentality that goes with it, is not all-pervasive, but, rather, is confined to the interstices between the islands of the family, the community and the voluntary association, where it is not the market but 'traditional', 'ethical' and 'Christian' principles that should hold sway. It is within these islands so the argument goes, that humanity can express its 'neediness' and vulnerability'—if necessary backed by the forces of the law.

Secondly they may admit the limitation in their own purely *a priori* account of human beings, but attempt to show that the *a posteriori* results of creating a society in the image of liberal man are in fact more conducive to satisfying our 'vulnerable' and 'needy' sides than any non-liberal alternative available, even those which start from the premises of 'neediness' and 'vulnerability'. The argument is a familiar one that has been with us in a fully-developed form from at least the time of Vilfredo Pareto,[3] who argued that the self-seeking of each can, in appropriate market conditions, lead to certain optimal results in which no one is worse off and at least some people are better off. Better this, it is argued, than a 'caring' but stagnant society that can help no one. A modern version of it is to be found in the way Nigel Lawson used the Laffer curve in some of his budgets to legitimate sharply regressive tax-cuts: lower rates of tax will lead to growth, and thus to higher tax revenues which can be used to reduce the burden of taxation on everyone.

If this increases the wealth of society, so the argument goes, it frees us up to use the state to introject 'neediness' and 'vulnerability' into the market place itself. All kinds of 'neediness' can be addressed in this manner, some of which are of a purely material kind like social security benefits, which might not seem to contradict at least the spirit of Susan Mendus's account. But it seems to apply to other needs too. For it is not the case that the values and dimensions of human life that centrally occupy her have no material or institutional embodiment. Often they do, and the state's ability to affect this material embodiment, affects also the spiritual emanations that they produce.

For a current example consider the Hospice movement. Run in the main by religious orders, their purpose is to create humane conditions in which people at the end of their lives can both die and at the same time make sense of their own death—quintessentially therefore, they allow us to give voice to our vulnerability and our inability to control the world. They are also partly funded by the state, and it is this funding which determines the number of people they are able to admit. A higher funding—other things being equal—increases the proportion of human activity that society devotes to recognizing that dimension of human nature which is represented by our 'vulnerability', and therefore, accordingly, reduces the proportion devoted to giving the 'independent' and 'controlling' sides of our natures their head.

Now it is clear that if this example stands up, it would suggest that liberals might have a general answer to Susan Mendus's account. However large the proportion of human activity that goes on expressing man's 'vulnerable' side should be, other things being equal the wealthiest society will be the one that is most able to provide it. Therefore, so the argument goes, we should both encourage everyone to make it the wealthiest society while having the wisdom to use this

[3] R. Cirillo, *The Economics of Vilfredo Pareto* (London: Frank Cass, 1979).

wealth—via the state if necessary—in accordance with our real human natures.

The liberal account has it that only by thinking of ourselves as primarily 'controlling' and 'invulnerable' can we create a genuinely free market, and only by creating such a market can we generate the wealth and space that we need to nurture, support, and make room for our vulnerabilities adequately. The argument suggests that even if we think that 'vulnerability' is the most important feature of humanity, none the less we still need to support as primary a conception of man that explicitly excludes it.

According to this defence, the primary notion of man has to exclude the vulnerable dimension not on any *a priori* grounds of its relative importance to us as human beings, but because it is needed to create the foundations for the best functioning *society* and *economy* for fulfilling the needs of vulnerable man. Philosophical conceptions of mankind do not automatically create the conditions for their own fulfilment in real societies; they are always mediated by the structure of the society in question. So even if we were to believe, for instance, that Sophocles has a more complete account of human beings than someone like Adam Smith, one might still conclude that a society made in the image of Smithian man was *more* likely to recognize, and allow us to express, our vulnerable sides than the empoverished, slave-dependent, woman subjugating society made in the image of man to be found in Sophocles or Aristotle, which does not recognize the great majority as being proper people at all—let alone recognizing their vulnerabilities.

This line of thinking makes me somewhat sceptical about discussing liberal man in any manner that abstracts him from liberal society itself. The danger is that of an essentialist or abstractionist reduction of something that is real, complex, concrete, and historically produced. It suggests also that liberalism has a certain defence in depth that comes from its integration of philosophy, politics and economics, and that the purely philosophical objections which now follow (and also, for that matter, the different objections which Susan Mendus herself advances), would need an equivalent grounding outside of philosophy before they can confront liberalism on equal terms.

That, of course, is outside the scope of this paper. In what follows I shall be looking at the concept of liberal man confined, as it is in Susan Mendus's account to the terrain of philosophy. My purpose is not to deny the significance of the above points, but rather to show how hard this line of argument is going to have to work to overcome the philosophical objections to the concept of liberal man that now follow.

Fixed vulnerabilities and plastic vulnerabilities

So far we have not challenged the counterposition of the 'controlling' or 'self-directing' sides of our nature to the 'needy' or 'vulnerable' sides, which Susan Mendus takes for granted. It is time to look at these concepts, because a closer examination reveals a more complex picture. Is it a vulnerability to *other people* and a neediness for them which is at issue here, or is it a vulnerability to such things as death, human insignificance in the immensity of time and space, etc.— the sorts of thing that form the point of departure of, for instance, Pascal's *Pensées*[4]—in which case it is, broadly speaking a vulnerability to nature?

With some of the examples that Susan Mendus cites, it is difficult to make this distinction very clearly. With Greek tragedy, for instance, it is by its very nature impossible to do so: on the one hand the concept of the person is never that of the isolated individual but is one of a bearer of specific roles within the polis, on the other hand the path of this role-bearer is characteristically barred by Fate or the Gods—by something which stands outside both ourselves and other people. So in this example the two sorts of vulnerability are intertwined. But elsewhere it is possible to be more specific about whether the vulnerability is to other people—henceforth 'sociovulnerability'—or to something beyond them—henceforth 'naturavulnerability'. In her paper, for example, Susan Mendus has the following to say about John Steinbeck's *The Grapes of Wrath*:

Steinbeck's major novels, written in the late 1930s and early 1940s, make constant reference to the coming of the machine, and to the ways in which the machine destroys the American Dream of endeavour rewarded. *The Grapes of Wrath* is, of course, the most obvious place where antagonism between man and machine is discussed. The Joads of Oklahoma are the victims of a burgeoning technology which denies them their birthright of a chicken in every pot and a car in every garage. As 'man' becomes more powerful over nature, individual men become impotent, or they become 'machine men'. Steinbeck speaks of 'the machine man, driving a dead tractor on land he does not know and love, [he] understands only chemistry; and he is contemptuous of the land and of himself. When the corrugated iron doors are shut, he goes home, and his home is not the land'.

The pursuit of technological supremacy—of control over nature—makes man less human. The analogy now is not between man as one thing in nature, like the vine tree. Rather the analogy is between man and the things which tame nature—the tractor, the machinery of the new technology. Man is no longer a part of the natural world, but a being distinct from the natural world, who manipulates it for his own purposes.[5]

[4] *Pensées* (Harmondsworth: Penguin, 1976).
[5] See above 51.

Peter Binns

Here the dehumanization is seen as following from the loss of our vulnerability to the *forces of nature*. Yet this is a curious interpretation both of the events in question and Steinbeck's own intentions. For the Joads have *lost control* of their own little patch of nature; their reduction to casual labourers on exploitative Californian farms making them even more vulnerable to the vaguaries of the market for employment. It is bizarre to see this in terms of an *increasing invulnerability*. What has gone wrong?

The simplest and most obvious answer is to say that the Joads are indeed more vulnerable after than before, and that they are even less in control of their own world, but the nature of this vulnerability has changed. Before they were vulnerable to a *lesser* degree and more by *natural* forces; after they were vulnerable to a *greater* degree and by more *social* forces. The confusion seems to have arisen from not fully recognizing the different sources from which this vulnerability can derive, and from seeing any diminution of vulnerability to nature as meaning, *ipso facto*, a diminution of all vulnerabilities—which is just not the case.[6]

This combination of factors is not at all unusual, in fact it is difficult to see how it could be otherwise. If the balance between my vulnerability to and my control over nature shifts towards the latter, then it would seem to follow that less of my energy needs to be devoted towards extracting a living from a decreasingly niggardly nature, and, as a corollary, there are more ways I can use nature to help, harm, or otherwise affect my neighbour. Naturavulnerability and sociovulnerability would, therefore, on this view, tend to vary inversely with respect to each other. Also one would expect there to be a secular shift towards the latter as technology develops over time, though the permanencies of the human condition—our biological form, the necessity of death, our central psychical needs—will prescribe a lower limit beneath which our naturavulnerability cannot be pushed.

But there is no necessary connection between decreasing naturavulnerability and increasing dehumanization, as Susan Mendus

[6] Later on in her paper she offers a different and more plausible account: 'There are forms of dependence which assert our value as human beings, and there are forms of dependence which deny it. The dependence which implies that, as human beings, we have only an instrumental value is the worst form of dependence. It is this which is implied in the move from an analogy between man and the natural world to an analogy between man and the inanimate objects of the new technology.' This seems to me to be entirely correct. But she immediately goes on to say: 'It is the very rejection of dependency (the neediness and vulnerability of the vine tree) which brings with it the denial of humanity.' This does not at all follow, and it immediately returns us to her original argument which, as I have argued above, is not at all convincing.

seems to suggest. There is nothing about a machine which could possibly have any such consequences; after all if a new machine becomes available which can increase my productive efficiency, this does not, in and of itself, take away any of my old options: I can still go on having exactly the same relationship to nature if I want, it is just that I do not have to, and this can hardly be called 'dehumanization'. The machine does not make me do anything, though it may require increased wisdom from me if I am to use it intelligently.

But of course this a long way from the picture that Steinbeck gives us. The Joads and other dustbowl Okies had no such options, but that is because they were not, as Susan Mendus claims, involved with an 'antagonism between man and machine'. Instead, they were involved, via the operations of the market, in a struggle with other *men*, who, because of their access to major capital sources, could afford the economies of scale and the machinery to defeat them. Any other view gives rise to an illusory anthropomorphization of dead machines, a view which is no less illusory for being embedded in the legends (but not the reality) surrounding such figures as Ned Ludd and John Henry.

So to explain what is going on in *The Grapes of Wrath*, we should not concentrate on the by-product of a decreasing vulnerability to nature; instead we should see it in terms of the Joads' *increasing vulnerability to other people*. And this entirely inverts Susan Mendus's claim that 'dehumanization' is to be correlated with invulnerability. If we are to continue thinking of their fate as a dehumanizing one, then, in this case at least, we shall have to connect dehumanization with increasing vulnerability instead.

Looking at the different varieties of vulnerability in this way adds a further twist to the notions of 'control' and 'self-direction' with which they are contrasted in Susan Mendus's account. I am vulnerable to death from old age in a quite different way from the way the Joads were vulnerable to changing market conditions. The former I have to accept as an inevitability, and one of the particular strengths of Susan Mendus's account is that it provides us with a good way of assimilating this rationally, pointing to the things that are uniquely available to us because of our mortality (we can for instance celebrate our ability to empathize with the figures in tragic literature and thank God that we are neither animals that have no language, nor Angels for whom death is not a possible experience). But nothing like this attaches to the *The Grapes of Wrath* example, or indeed any example where the vulnerability is created by, and removable by, human beings acting together—i.e. where it is *socioplastic*.

The Joads are, certainly, victims, but as part of the human race they are also the potential agents for changing the circumstances that made them thus vulnerable. In such cases it is never enough to say that they are *just* victims. We are not just the victims of historical conditions, but, in the long run at least, the authors of historical conditions too.

For there is a large portion of our sociovulnerabilities—arguably all of them—whose socioplasticities are revealed through history, anthropology, sociology and psychology: we can describe the historical, cultural, social or psychological conditions through which our sociovulnerabilites can be changed, modulated, restructured and mediated, and there is an important sense in which it is up to us to decide whether or not to do so. Consider an example from psychology: Freud considered the Oedipus Complex to be an inescapable drama through which each child must pass in the journey to adulthood. Let us suppose that this is a correct description of contemporary western societies; it is still open to argue, as Malinowski did,[7] that in different social circumstances—those of the Trobriand islanders for instance—it can be avoided altogether. And if he is right, from this it would follow that there exists a recipe for eliminating the Oedipal stage in any place that chooses to copy the Trobriand islanders in the relevant respects.

It may be argued that the notion of socioplasticity is excessively wide here. Is it really open to us to reverse the trend to urbanization, let alone to return to the subsistence economy of tropical islanders? Surely we need a more restricted notion that discounts the alternatives which produce excessively high costs?

I think this would be a mistake. This is not because I share any of these utopian illusions, but because I believe retaining a wide definition points to an important truth, namely that societies, together with the social norms and the human natures that they produce, are themselves the historical product of the conscious actions of people in the past (though not necessarily their intended consequences), and therefore society's future is a result of our actions now. The notion is an empowering one, therefore; it makes us take responsibility for our world—instead of accepting it as an alien object it makes it possible for us either to endorse it positively or alternatively to actively seek to change it.

Individualism and collectivism

I also want to stress this point to contrast it with Susan Mendus's position, which seems to me to have opposed implications. As I have said before, I think she is entirely right to see our vulnerability and neediness as a necessary part of our nature and as something to be celebrated rather than regarded as an unfortunate weakness. The trouble is that she seems too ready to concede to this part of our nature things which have no real place there.

[7] *Sex and Repression in Savage Society* (London: Kegan Paul, 1927).

But this gives no succour to liberals, because in so far as she underestimates our ability to change the world around us, or seems too reluctant to allow that this can sometimes count *against* dehumanization, the sorts of control it produces fit uneasily into the conception of liberal man. For the very notion of 'socioplasticity' cannot, on the liberal conception, be allowed anything other than a derivative existence: unless socioplasticities can be reduced or otherwise explained, via appropriate methodological individualist procedures, to things which are purely *individuoplastic*, the liberal must deny either that they exist, or, if they do exist, that they are significant.

This is not a question to which there can be any *a priori* answers; nonetheless, a *prima facie* case can be made out against liberalism on the basis of the existence of our vulnerabilities—both social and individual—and the socioplastic character of the sources of, and the solutions for these vulnerabilities. Only the briefest outline of such an argument can be given here, but the method is a general one and we can at least show how it might be extended.

We can divide up actions into three main categories: (A_1) those which are performed by subjects who are purely autonomous individuals; (A_2) those performed by collective subjects of one sort or another; and (A_3) hybrids of A_1 and A_2 actions. In practice it is very difficult to find examples of pure A_1 actions; even that paradigm of individualism, the purchase of a commodity in a free market, is not quite so simple as it seems: most consumer goods are purchased by families for families from a family wage, and almost all producer goods are bought by that quintessence of collectivism, the corporation or company. So even within the marketplace A_1 actions are in the minority. Outside it they are even thinner on the ground: when I play football there are certainly some individual actions implied—joining the team, turning up on the day, agreeing to play in a certain position, etc.—but it is only in so far as I am part of a collective entity, the team, that I can play the game or win the match. The same can be said, *mutatis mutandis*, for many other activities: participating in a seminar, deciding upon some action as a member of a club or political party, making love, and so on. These are all A_3 actions—they are mixtures of collective and individual actions—but in each of these examples the collective element is dominant.

If liberalism has to defend a conception of man as defined essentially by A_1 actions, it has to account for the *prima facie* implausibility of this account given how thin on the ground A_1 actions seem to be. If the real me is given by A_1 actions, then, against all appearances to the contrary, an awful lot of A_2 and A_3 actions will have to turn out to be A_1 actions underneath. Worse still, when we attempt to use this notion to do political work, it seems even more implausible. For the actions that we can most readily concede to be A_1 actions are those that seem to

69

characterize me much more personally than politically; they include such things as going for a walk, praying, reading a book, and so on, and it would be difficult to think of these things characterizing—let alone forming the basis—of fundamental *political* differences between societies.

Indeed, once we look at things from a specifically political direction, the individual element in, for instance, A_3 type actions seems to diminish markedly. For societies are not optional in the way that football teams are. There is nothing remotely equivalent—except in very marginal cases—to the personal choice involved in participating in a football team when it comes to the state. The state has a juridical monopoly which I simply cannot choose to exempt myself from. In so far as a concept of liberty is appropriate here, it will of necessity be socioplastic rather than individuoplastic in form.

If there is an inherent implausibility in the notion of liberal man, it would seem to me to be more located in this lacuna in the explanation of the social part of ourselves than in the notions of 'neediness' and 'vulnerability' that Susan Mendus refers to. The latter seem, rather, to be somewhat ambiguous notions; there is a perfectly correct sense in which the whole of the social dimension of our existence can be seen as ways in which we are all, as individuals, vulnerable to other people, and if this is what Susan Mendus has in mind, she is quite right to see it as part of our particular excellence as human beings. But in that case it is wrong to see this as sanctioning a celebration of human powerlessness.

What has happened here is a conflation of two quite distinct category pairs. We can contrast our neediness and vulnerability with our controlling or self-directing sides, but we can also contrast our existence *qua* individuals with our existence *qua* participants in collective activity and experiences. If we fail to make the latter distinction alongside the former, we will be led to miscategorize important aspects of human life. All examples of our *collective powers* will, on this view, appear simply as *individual impotences*; instead of showing us where this power lies, it will falsely suggest that we have none, that all there is left for us to do is to celebrate this supposed fact.

It seems to offer us a choice between only two alternatives; on the one hand the liberal man who, in trying to gain the whole world has lost his own place within it, and on the other hand the anti-liberal man who regains his place in the world by giving up many of his powers to change it. On the one hand, then, bumptious alienation, on the other, a de-powering counsel of despair.

The choice is a false one. By neglecting our collective human powers and implicitly conflating them with individual impotences, one ends up with a one-sided picture of human nature and of humans in nature. The portrait implies that we can only fulfil our natures by giving up some of our powers, that the only alternative to rampant liberal individualism is anti-liberal cosmic prostration. The alternatives are much wider than that.

In defence of powerfully co-vulnerable people

If the account we have been offered is too one-sided, what are the other sides that have been neglected or underdeveloped? If we accept the terms of reference and contrast 'control' with 'vulnerability', our two category pairs yield four combinations: (i) the controlling individual, (ii) the vulnerable individual, (iii) the controlling group or collective, and (iv) the vulnerable collective. In the last section of this paper I argued that Susan Mendus had overloaded the vulnerable combinations by conflating one of the controlling combinations, (iii), in with them. Here I want to argue that giving (iii) its proper place and status restores a better-balanced view of people and their relationship to the world around them. To do so it will be necessary to question her terms of reference which lead to a polarization between 'control' and 'vulnerability', but before we do that we need to return to the discussion of humanizing and dehumanizing activities that we encountered above around Steinbeck's *The Grapes of Wrath*. In Steinbeck's account, the defeat of the Joads by the new men with their chemicals and tractors is, as Susan Mendus correctly states, a process of unequivocal dehumanization. But in what sense is it a defeat of 'vulnerability' by 'control'? In the earlier discussion I gave reasons for thinking that it was not; here I want to look at it from a different direction.

There is an important sense in which the question is misconceived. Both the Joads and their 'machine men' successors had control of the land in so far as it was they who farmed the land, not the land that farmed them. But both did so within definitely limited conditions, and these changing conditions gave rise to a changing set of vulnerabilities for each of them, as we have seen. In so far as the Joads were dehumanized it was because they were deprived from occupying their earlier position of controlling their own patch of land. With the 'machine men' it might appear to be the other way about; given Susan Mendus's account one might draw the conclusion that they were dehumanized by having an *excessive* control over nature. But that is not really a credible stand to take. We have seen above that technological advance in itself merely creates new options for us. Since we can always go on choosing the old options if we want to, it can take nothing away from us.

At this point one might rightly object that no such 'choices' were in fact made by the 'machine men'. They were no more able to 'choose' the way of life of the Joads than the Joads were. Tractors, chemicals and an instrumental attitude to the land were a necessary consequence of external constraints: capital markets, commodity prices and so on. But these markets and prices, coercive and inhuman though their workings might be, derive this coercive power not from Fate or an unyielding nature, but from forms of *human activity*. When it is claimed that the 'machine men' had no choice but to operate in the way they did, then the implication must be that they had no plausible way—in the historical circumstances in question—to prevent their descent into being mere adjuncts of machines.

Under such circumstances, where it seems hopeless to resist, it is very easy to construe the constraining forces as deriving from a super-human or extrahuman source, even though they originate in human activity, and generally can, in the appropriate historical circumstances, be undone by human activity as well. Furthermore there is a danger in taking circumstances when people rightly believe there to be no socioplastic alternative open to them as the paradigm case for the human condition. For the roots of the most potent social forces are very deep indeed; they have their origins and draw their nurture from the most obscure and humble sources in the lives of people. Most, like the spark that led the crowd to storm the Bastille 200 years ago, are lost in the obscurity of history; others can be traced to a more personal source. The current national and international wave of resistance to the destruction of the Brazilian Amazon, for instance, thus flows in part from the murder of Chico Mendez, hitherto an obscure organizer of rubber-tappers who refused to be intimidated by landed interests.

This example is interesting because it shows the need to maintain the sharp separation mentioned above between the vulnerable individual and the social group with the potentiality for a degree of social power. It is perfectly correct to see Chico Mendez as individually vulnerable to his murderers, but if we leave out of the picture the social power generated by his martyrdom, we have only told a part of the story; we shall see him only as a *victim*, even though a most important part of his life was the *power* that he shared with others to generate a significant social force.

This account helps to explain what otherwise might seem irrational. If we ask why, rationally, the person *qua* individual is prepared to risk martyrdom, the reply might be that he was following his conscience, that his very authenticity as a person was at stake, that he was not prepared to go on living with himself if he was not prepared to take the risk, and so on. Such a reply, taken on its own, is odd. It would suggest that an ex-person—albeit an authentic ex-person—is a better thing to be than a real person with all its potentialities for life and action. It suggests an irresoluable conflict between self and conscience. It would be much more plausible to broaden the account, to identify the self not just with an individual, but with something wider in appropriate circumstances. As an individual it makes much less sense to risk martyrdom than it does as a rubber-tapper, a worker, a Brazilian, or especially a member of humanity as a whole. In so far as Chico Mendez was able to see himself as any of these things, to that extent he would have had more reason to take the risk. Suppose, for instance, he saw himself in the front-line of the battle of humanity against deforestation and the possibly catastrophic consequences of the greenhouse effect that it would produce. Taking the risk might seem an acceptable cost for the possibility of improving the chances for one's children and the rest of humanity in the future.

Within this context one can make sense of 'conscience' and 'authenticity' as pertaining to the self *qua* individual, but what makes them rational voices that it is worth listening to is the fact that they supervene on those parts of the self that go beyond the individual. It is only because people really are collective as well as individual entities—their essence as persons is defined in terms of A_2 and A_3 actions as well as A_1 actions—that it makes sense to listen to the voice of this wider self and the reasons that it provides us with.

If there is a fundamental problem with the notion of liberal man, it is surely to be located here. For liberals all collectivities of people have a secondary ontological status: in the real world, they believe, all collectivities can be thought of as reducible to individuals without remainder. Yet if this is true one consequence will be to remove the thing that makes the voice of 'conscience' and 'authenticity' worth listening to for the primary individuals who form the basic parameters of explanation on the liberal account.

This is where a real alternative to liberal man can be developed from, though it is beyond the scope of this paper to do so here. From our point of view, however, the main point is this. This critique of liberalism can only be formulated by confronting the central liberal notion of the self as a pure individual, and showing how only a much broader notion makes sense of some of the variety of human experience.

Because this social or collective dimension of the self is not apparent in Susan Mendus's conceptual tools, it is missed in her account. She seems, rather, to implicitly endorse the identification of the self with the individual, proposing instead an enriched notion of what the individual consists of. No doubt she would argue that the paticular features she draws attention to cannot easily be accommodated into the liberal account, but it seems just as plausible to argue the other way about: to suggest that her modifications are minor and assimilable, and that they constitute a reaffirmation of the individualism of liberal man, even while putting a limit on his controlling side.

Furthermore there are real problems involved with the counterposition of the 'controlling' to the 'vulnerable', and in particular with failing to specify what the ground might look like in between or from side to side. As we have seen already, the reason why Susan Mendus sees the 'machine men' in *The Grapes of Wrath* as being less human is that they have more control over nature, and I have indicated what I believe is wrong with this account. But these problems have a conceptual source too; quite simply much too much is being forced to fit into a misplaced dichotomy between 'control' and 'vulnerability'.

'Vulnerability' indicates an openness to forces in the external world, and it can of course be contrasted with 'invulnerability'; but this is not the only way to prevent 'control' by the outside force. For the 'vulnerable' party may also be able to exert itself on the external force in a comparable or equivalent manner. Such a situation of co-vulnerability implies not 'control' but a *mutual power* to penetrate the other. In such a situation power and vulnerability co-vary: the more power people have, the more vulnerable they become to each other. But the greater this power the less is the *control* that anyone has over anyone else.

So to admit to our vulnerability is not at all to proclaim our powerlessness. To say that our vulnerability is one of the quintessential things that make us human, as Susan Mendus rightly does, is not at all to celebrate human powerlessness. In fact, since the major source of our vulnerability is other people, it is a reminder of the quite frightening power that we do actually possess to affect others. Such a situation cannot coexist with 'control', of course, and if there is 'control' then the situation has changed in a dehumanizing direction.

Liberal man is conceived of very differently. The good life consists of autonomizing the individual. Freedom means preventing others from penetrating this individual at all, except, perhaps, at the margin.

If 'power' and 'control' are collapsed into one, as they seem to be on both the liberal's and Susan Mendus's account, we shall be faced with an impossible choice. We can either be de-humanized and autonomized controllers of nature as with the liberal, or, as with Susan Mendus, we can be human through being vulnerable, but when we are vulnerable we will have to give up our power. Neither alternative looks very appetizing.

Naturalizing humans and humanizing nature

According to the position that I am advancing here, then, both these accounts depend on a false counterposition of 'vulnerability' to 'control'. This can be illustrated further by the problems that they encounter when conceiving of the relationship between people and nature. If the only way I can be vulnerable to nature is by being controlled by it, then I can only conceive of nature as in some way hostile to human beings and their activity. Nature will appear as an alien force from which humanity has been excluded. In such a situation all human power in nature will be 'unnatural' and all natural power which affects human beings will be 'inhuman'.

This is not at all the picture that Susan Mendus wants to create. Indeed when she refers to it directly, it is clear that she intends quite the opposite, with people as fully naturalized components of the cosmos. But to achieve this an altogether richer set of concepts is needed. For it is clear that 'vulnerability' and 'control' will not do the trick on their own. On the contrary only something like the notions we have referred to already—'mutual power' and 'co-vulnerability'—can begin to capture not just an important truth about the relationship of people to each other, but also the relationship between all of humanity to the rest of the natural world. Furthermore it would be a mistake to model this truth on portrayals of the human condition to be found in tragic literature, for these are characteristically drawn around circumstances in which such power is missing.

For liberal man it is not just that these concepts are absent, but also that the central theoretical framework seems to exclude them. The very notion of negative liberty implies that freedom is to be identified not with any mutuality in people's power but rather with the kind of relatively invulnerable power that quite properly can be called 'control'. So other individuals appear as alien on this picture, and, *a fortiori*, nature appears as dehumanized and human beings as unnatural.

Given this conception it is not surprising that for the liberal such things as protecting the ecosystem, if they are acknowledged at all, are not seen as following from the sorts of beings we are—powerful, co-vulnerable (and therefore potentially loving and nurturing) parts of nature—but rather as *secondary* to, and providing *overhead* costs for an isolated, acquisitive, controlling individual.

If we make people in this image, we should not be surprised if these secondary mechanisms—which are elaborately designed to keep such chaotic individuals from destroying their environment and each other—sometimes break down. Nor should we be surprised if these individuals find their world bereft of spiritual meaning and in need of a transcendent God to make good this lack.

Equally, it would be a mistake to believe that an adequate alternative to liberal man can be found by implicitly accepting the liberal notion of the individual (however non-controlling this individual might be) instead of a wider, more collective conception of what is involved in being a person. And it would be even more of a mistake to believe that only by de-powering people can one begin to construct a plausible alternative to liberal man.

Whether the synthesis of the liberal concept of man with the economic theory of market capitalism in which it is grounded can ever provide a comfortable home for such a concept of co-vulnerable, mutually powerful and needy human beings, is, of course, another matter. I personally do not believe that it can, but to argue the case would take us beyond this present paper, and, indeed, beyond philosophy.

Equality

DAVID MILLER*

I

It is a distinctive and unprecedented feature of modern societies that the idea of equality should hold a central place in their political thinking. I want to begin my enquiry by considering why this should be and what its significance is. For if there is indeed an important sense in which egalitarianism is written in to contemporary conditions of life, it makes no sense to think of oneself as taking a stand for or against equality. Now to say this is not to deny the equally inescapable fact that the issue of equality rouses fierce ideological passions between those who might describe themselves on one side as its friends and on the other as its enemies. But my suggestion is that both sides may misunderstand their contest. Their conflict is not about the value of equality as such, but about competing specifications of that value, about different versions of what it means to treat people as equals.

That this is so was suggested by one of the most profound observers of nineteenth-century society, Alexis de Tocqueville, who claimed in the Introduction to his classic work *Democracy in America* that:

> The gradual development of the principle of equality is, therefore, a providential fact. It has all the chief characteristics of such a fact: it is universal, it is lasting, it constantly eludes all human interference, and all events as well as all men contribute to its progress . . . those who have fought for it and even those who have declared themselves its opponents have all been driven along in the same direction, have all laboured to one end; some unknowingly and some despite themselves, all have been blind instruments in the hand of God.[1]

For Tocqueville this meant that the issue facing his generation was not whether or not to choose equality, but which kind of equality to choose: equal freedom or equal surrender to despotic power. Now as I shall argue in a moment, the terms of this choice will vary historically and may not be precisely the same for us today as they were for Tocqueville

---

[1] A. de Tocqueville, *Democracy in America* (New York: Vintage Books, 1945), Vol. I, 6.

* I should like to thank Jerry Cohen and Michael Walzer for their very helpful comments on an earlier version of this paper.

David Miller

in 1835. What I wish to endorse is the way that he poses the issue of equality, as a question that is inescapably pressed upon us by the circumstances of modern society, but whose answer remains open and subject to political choice.

I also wish to commend Tocqueville's insight into the progressive character of equality. The history of egalitarianism is essentially a record of ideas that were at first visionary, then fiercely contested, then finally taken for granted as received wisdom. Examples spring readily to mind. At the time when, as the Archbishop of Lyons is reputed to have put it, if five men were gathered together it would be no surprise if each of them obeyed a different law,[2] the ideal of equality before the law—of a unified legal system which applied the same set of general rules to every member of society—would have seemed a mad utopian dream. By the nineteenth century legal equality was universally accepted (in theory if not always in practice), whereas political equality had reached the point of contentiousness. A sober liberal like J. S. Mill could write:

> I do not look upon equal voting as among the things which are good in themselves, provided they can be guarded against inconveniences. I look upon it as only relatively good; less objectionable than inequality of privilege grounded on irrelevant or adventitious circumstances, but in principle wrong, because recognizing a wrong standard, and exercising a bad influence on the voter's mind.[3]

More flamboyantly, Macaulay predicted that if universal suffrage were adopted ' . . . in two or three hundred years, a few lean and half naked fishermen may divide with owls and foxes the ruins of the greatest of European cities—may wash their nets amidst the relics of her gigantic docks, and build their huts out of the capitals of her stately cathedrals.'[4] To our contemporaries, even the most conservative among them, these views are only of antiquarian interest. *Of course* we all now believe in political equality, at least at the level of formal voting rights.

It is worth reminding ourselves that forms of equality we now take for granted were once contentious because it shows that 'egalitarianism' is a shifting target. 'The egalitarian' is the person who, on the issue under dispute, favours equality rather than differentiation. In the

[2] M. Bloch, *Feudal Society* (London: Routledge and Kegan Paul, 1965), Vol. I, 111.

[3] J. S. Mill, *Considerations on Representative Government*, in *Utilitarianism; On Liberty; Representative Government*, H. B. Acton ed. (London: Dent, 1972), 288.

[4] T. B. Macaulay, 'Mill's Essay on Government: Utilitarian Logic and Politics', in J. Lively and J. Rees (eds), *Utilitarian Logic and Politics* (Oxford: Clarendon Press, 1978), 122.

dispute between Macaulay and the older Mill on the extension of the franchise, the latter was 'the egalitarian', even though we might now regard him as hopelessly elitist and sexist. There is no single cause that egalitarians favour, no one motive that drives them to the views they hold. In liberal and conservative rhetoric, by contrast, 'the egalitarian' takes on a definite character. For instance:

> The fanatical egalitarian . . . will tend to wish so to condition human beings that the highest degree of equality of natural properties is achieved, the greatest degree of mental and physical, that is to say, total uniformity—which alone will effectively preserve society, as far as possible, from the growth of inequalities of whatever kind.[5]

What is wrong with this is that it presents 'the egalitarian' as possessed of an overpowering drive to eliminate differentiation of all conceivable kinds. But the construct is an imaginary one. The point I have been labouring is that we are all egalitarians on some issues, inegalitarians on others. Within the context of any particular debate—say over the extension of the suffrage—it makes perfectly good sense to identify some participants as egalitarians and others as not; but it is absurd to impute to the former the general aim of eliminating difference.

I shall shortly try to identify the central issue that currently divides those we may call egalitarians from their opponents. But before doing so I want to address the third claim made by Tocqueville in the passage I cited earlier. Tocqueville claims not only that the principle of equality is inescapable and progressive in its application, but that this is a 'providential fact'. I do not know whether we are to take his allusion to divine agency literally or metaphorically. What is clear is that Tocqueville saw the movement towards greater equality of condition as going on behind men's backs and independently of their will, but he does not try to explain the mechanism involved. Can we do better than him here? Do modern societies have common features that explain why they, but not earlier forms of human association, are driven in an egalitarian direction? Or is there indeed one particular feature that sufficiently explains this fact?

It is possible that our egalitarianism is overdetermined. Ernest Gellner, in a wide-ranging analysis, points to no less than fourteen aspects of advanced industrial societies which he believes help to foster equality.[6] However, I think there is reason to pay special attention to a determinant that does not feature specifically in Gellner's list, although

[5] I. Berlin, 'Equality', *Proceedings of the Aristotelian Society*, 56 (1955–6), 314.
[6] E. Gellner, 'The Social Roots of Egalitarianism', in *Culture, Identity and Politics* (Cambridge: Cambridge University Press, 1987).

it stands behind a number that do, namely the market economy. Without attempting to disentangle the very complex relationship between the emergence of market relations and the achievement of various forms of equality, such as equality before the law,[7] I want to suggest that a society in which markets occupy a central place will inevitably generate an egalitarian ethos, which in turn will receive formal expression in social and political philosophy.

Why should this be? An essential property of market relations is their abstract character. Buyer and seller meet in the market simply as bearers of commodities and money. As individuals, they may of course have personal relations of other kinds, but these are irrelevant at the point of exchange. All that matters here is the value that they have to offer, whether this takes the form of money, an article for sale, or their services. And under normal circumstances (barring fraud, etc.) the value contributed by each party will be approximately the same. Thus insofar as the exchange relationship is also a social relationship, the parties to it must consider themselves, and be considered by others, to be equals. This point was classically formulated by Karl Marx:

> The subjects in exchange exist for one another only through these equivalents [their exchange values], as of equal worth, and prove themselves to be such through the exchange of the objectivity in which the one exists for the other. Since they only exist for one another in exchange in this way, as equally worthy persons, possessors of equivalent things, who thereby prove their equivalence, they are, as equals, at the same time also indifferent to one another; whatever other individual distinction there may be does not concern them; they are indifferent to all their other individual peculiarities.[8]

Later he expresses the same idea more concretely:

> A worker who buys commodities for 3s. appears to the seller in the same function, in the same equality—in the form of 3s.—as the king who does the same. All distinction between them is extinguished.[9]

Marx goes on to argue, characteristically, that egalitarian ideals—presumably he has in mind the ideas of the French Revolution, and of socialists who saw their work as carrying those ideas through to their

---

[7] What I have in mind is that some aspects of equality may be a precondition for the emergence of a market economy—for instance it is hard to see how a regime of free contract can work unless the contracting parties are all seen as bearers of the same set of basic personal and property rights. Although I draw attention to the influence of social practices on ideas, and cite Marx, I am very far from subscribing to any simple economic determinism.

[8] K. Marx, *Grundrisse* (Harmondsworth: Penguin, 1973), 242.

[9] Ibid., 246.

fulfilment—derive from and express the material equality of the exchange relationship.

Now the analysis I have just offered is subject to one very important qualification of which Marx himself was only too well aware. Market relations are from one point of view egalitarian, but from another point of view they are inegalitarian, inasmuch as the levels of benefit finally enjoyed by different individuals depend upon their assets and especially upon their productive capacities. Marx developed this into a theory of exploitation, but we do not need to follow him here. The essential point is that if we focus on *production* rather than *exchange*, we find unequally endowed individuals creating different amounts of value, and the market here becomes a device whereby this initial inequality is converted into a final inequality of consumption goods. This aspect of the market gives rise to a second, and potentially conflicting, set of ideals, centring on the notion of desert. Individuals perform differently, create unequal amounts of value, and as a result deserve unequal rewards.

So I want to say that market economies both generate wide-ranging ideas of equality and at the same time foster a different view which centres on the idea of desert. It would be wrong to say that the desert principle is inherently anti-egalitarian, for that depends on the context in which it is deployed. It can be used, for instance, to defend equality before the law, and also equality of opportunity, where this means the removal of external barriers to individual social mobility. Here desert and equality pull together. But in other contexts they begin to pull apart. This can be seen in nineteenth century arguments about political equality, where the view that each person has an equal entitlement to participate in government clashed with the view that people were qualified to rule in proportion to their competence.[10] It can be seen, too, in recent more radical developments of the idea of equality of opportunity which expand the range of external circumstances to be equalized in such a way that eventually there is no room left for desert to get a hold.[11] Indeed I believe it illuminating to see many contemporary disputes about equality as disputes about the respective ranges of the two principles: how far should our social arrangements treat people equally, and how far according to their (in practice substantially unequal) deserts?

[10] See my paper 'Democracy and Social Justice', *British Journal of Political Science*, **8** (1978), 1–19, reprinted in P. Birnbaum, J. Lively and G. Parry (eds), *Democracy, Consensus and Social Contract* (London: Sage, 1978).

[11] See J. Rawls, *A Theory of Justice* (Cambridge, Mass.: Harvard University Press, 1971), esp. sections 12 and 48; B. Williams, 'The Idea of Equality', in P. Laslett and W. G. Runciman (eds), *Philosophy, Politics and Society*, second series (Oxford: Blackwell, 1964).

David Miller

If we now ask about the substance of those disputes, I take the burning issue of our own period to be equality in the conditions of life. It is hard to specify what this means more precisely without begging the questions I want to discuss in the following two sections, but the general point is that whereas equality before the law, political equality, and equality of opportunity have all passed into the realm of received wisdom, issues such as equality of income and the equal provision of goods and services by agencies of the state remain deeply controversial. So we may identify contemporary egalitarians as those who in one way or another wish to see greater equality in the conditions of life, and anti-egalitarians as those who resist this impulse. But there is very substantial variety within both camps. I shall not here attempt to explore the many forms of anti-egalitarianism. Instead I shall examine some recent attempts to delineate the idea of equality of condition.

II

Let me begin this inquiry by drawing a distinction between simple and complex equality. An ideal of equality is simple when it specifies some characteristic X which is to be distributed equally among the population we are considering. Equality is realized insofar as everyone is equal in respect of X. 'X' might refer to income, property, welfare or whatever—there are as many versions of simple equality as there are characteristics which might form its basis (I shall examine some of the more plausible below).

Complex equality approaches the ideal in a different way. It recognizes a number of relevant dimensions along which individuals may be scored, but it does not insist that scores be equalized along any dimension in particular. Instead it claims that overall equality can be achieved by counterbalancing among the different dimensions. If the dimensions are independent, in the sense that there is no connection between how a person performs on one and how he performs on others, then relative gains in one direction can be set against relative losses in another. Now clearly what has to be shown here is how this complexity adds up to *equality*, and this is a question to which I shall return. For the present, I want simply to note that there may be conceptions of equality of condition that are not captured by the simple 'equality of X' formula.

Most recent discussion has, however, taken this formula as its starting point, and we must begin by asking whether any version of simple equality seems defensible as a social ideal. In pursuing this question I shall not be concerned with the difficulties that are frequently raised about the compatibility of equality with other values such as economic efficiency and personal liberty, important though these are politically. My line of attack will rather be to ask whether any of the conceptions under discussion seems persuasive as a conception of equality, given an intuitive sense of why equality matters.

Assuming, then, that our aim is to bring about greater equality in the material conditions of life, what kind of equality should we be trying to promote? Which basic principle should govern the allocation of specific rights, opportunities, resources, etc.? The answer that is likely to come to mind first is that we should aim for equality of well-being, where 'well-being' stands in for satisfaction, happiness, self-realization, or whatever concept is most adequately thought to capture the idea of how well someone's life is going in general.[12] Equality is not uniformity; people vary in their needs, preferences, ambitions, etc., so they should be allocated different specific items. The disabled person should have his wheelchair, the mountaineer his axe and ropes, the scholar his books. But the egalitarian's aim will be so to regulate these specific assignments that everyone ends up equally well-off, equally satisfied.

But for several reasons this answer seems not to be sustainable. One has to do with whether comparative judgments of welfare of the kind the equality principle requires can meaningfully be made. I am not here suggesting general scepticism as to whether we can ever know that A is happier than B. The problem seems rather to be this. Comparative judgments can most readily be made when what we are looking at is something like conscious states of pleasure; we often have a pretty good idea about whether Bill or Tom enjoyed the film more. But the judgments that equality of well-being requires us to make are of a far more abstract character. For we are supposed to be assessing lives from the inside, so to speak, judging how well a particular life is going by the standards the person himself would apply. If we use some more concrete criterion, such as pleasure, then we are loading the scales in favour of those who rate pleasure highly in their assessment of what makes life worth living, and against, say, monastics. But if we try to get at such an

---

[12] Why does this answer seem intuitively obvious as a starting point? The argument for it is that egalitarian policies are a way of showing equal concern and respect for each individual (see for instance R. Dworkin, 'Equality of Welfare', *Philosophy and Public Affairs*, **10** (1981), 185–246 and my own much briefer discussion in *Social Justice* (Oxford: Clarendon Press, 1976), Ch. 4, section 4). Since what ultimately matters to each indvidual is how well his life is going, i.e. his level of well-being, we manifest equal respect by ensuring that this level is as far as possible the same for everyone. (I do not now mean to endorse this argument—see my critical observations in 'Arguments for Equality', *Midwest Studies in Philosophy*, Vol. VII (Minneapolis: University of Minnesota Press, 1982)—but it seems to capture best the intuitive appeal of equality of well-being.)

David Miller

all-embracing idea of personal well-being, we not only face enormous
practical difficulties but some theoretical problems that may be insur-
mountable. For people's notions of the good life are very often
informed by social judgments—to take a very common instance, people
judge their own success by the relative standing they achieve on some
dimension such as income—and we might then be in the bizarrre
position, as egalitarians, of having to compensate people for losses of
well-being brought about by their own anti-egalitarian beliefs. These
and other internal difficulties for the equality of welfare idea have been
explored at some length by Dworkin in his paper of that title, and I have
little to add to his persuasive critique.

It may, however, be worth inserting an observation about the political implications of taking equality of well-being seriously and literally
as an ideal. Two consequences would follow. First, some agency—in
practice the state and its various branches—would need to gather
information about each person's welfare function in order to establish
what assignment of rights, etc. would implement equality of well-
being. Second, that assignment would stand in need of constant
revision as welfare functions changed, making it impossible to establish
a stable social order in which people could make firm judgments about
the resources that would be available to them in the future. Now in
reply it might be said that this does take the ideal too crudely and
literally, and with a reply of that sort I have some sympathy. (It
corresponds to the reply I often have to make to libertarian critics of the
very idea of social justice, for instance.) But the crude argument does
bring out one damaging feature of equality of well-being as a social
ideal, namely that it leaves no room for a distinction between private
and public. One may, that is to say, take a view of the following sort:
our social ideals should apply to the public allocation of rights and
resources, as carried out by the various institutions that together make
up a particular society. What private use individuals make of those
rights and resources is not in general a matter of public concern. I mean
to say by this both that, as a practical matter, the state should not seek to
inform itself about what it going on in the private sphere, or intervene
even with the aim of making people better at converting their resources
into welfare; and that, as a philosophical matter, we need some distinction between social ethics and personal morality. If you are messing
your life up and squandering your talents, I may quite properly hector
you in the name of some moral beliefs that we both share, but it does not
follow that I should make a *social* judgment that this is a poor state of
affairs, provided of course that you have received your proper quota of
resources to dissipate.

For a number of reasons this public/private distinction cannot be
made watertight; but it is one thing to say that we may collectively
sometimes have an interest in a person's private choice of ends, and

another to say that personal well-being is the right stuff from which to coin social principles. Equality of well-being, to repeat, if taken literally would destroy the public/private distinction both in theory and in practice, and I take that to be a strong argument against it.

Perhaps the most potent part of the argument concerns personal choice. The amount of well-being that any given person extracts from an assignment of resources will depend on the choices he makes; in particular, he may lower the level he would otherwise receive by making bad choices. For instance he may stake half his monthly salary on Likely Lad in the 3.30 at Cheltenham, and be forced to live on bread and water thereafter. Or, through carelessness, he may book a much needed annual holiday in a half-built hotel where the disco plays throughout the night. Or again, to take a case discussed by Dworkin, he may decide to acquire an expensive taste, like ocean racing, satisfying which requires a disproportionate sacrifice of resources. In none of these cases does it seem plausible to say that the loss of welfare which results from the choice should be made good by supplying the person in question with additional resources from the social pool. If equality of welfare is a way of showing equal concern for each person, then we do that by providing the appropriate share of resources in the first place, and to make good the effects of personal choice no matter what is to count this person twice over at the expense of others whose welfare must be lowered by the compensatory transfer.

To this it might be said that the 'appropriate' share of our profligate cannot be calculated without taking into account his propensity for big bets on the horses and so forth. But to say that would be to deny personal responsibility entirely, and I do not believe egalitarians will want to take that course. They will stand ready to compensate people for personal characteristics that are innate or acquired unwittingly, but not for the direct effects of their choices. This, then, is enough to sink any straightforward commitment to equality of welfare.[13]

[13] An interesting side question is whether one can recognize the significance of choice in this way without abandoning egalitarianism altogether. If we say that people should bear the costs and benefits of the choices they make about their use of resources, shouldn't we also respect the choices they make about the *disposition* of those resources? Musn't we allow departures from equality through gift, transfer, and so forth. In other words, if you allow that choices must count in the course of abandoning equality of welfare, don't you end up with Nozick? The brief answer to this is that the choices we have been discussing are private choices, in the sense of choices which affect only the welfare of the chooser and do not impinge upon the social allocation of rights and benefits. Nozick's trick is to disguise the social nature of other sorts of choice by concentrating on individual cases; for instance he talks about a particular A and a particular B exchanging services rather than about a general

David Miller

If we abandon equality of well-being, what alternative is there? The foregoing argument suggests that we need to get back from well-being itself to the stuff from which it is derived, which in a very wide sense we may label resources. So the alternative to equality of well-being appears to be some version of equality of resources, where resources will have to include both welfare-inducing features of the external environment and personal capacities, such as mental and physical abilities.

Let us concentrate first on external resources, and ask the two most obvious questions, namely, what shall count as a resource, and, how shall we decide when resources are equally distributed among a given population? Take the second question first. The simplest answer would be to say that resources are equally distributed when everyone has access to an identical bundle; in other words, everything in our universe of distribution is divided up into n identical parcels and handed out one to each person. But to prescribe this as a solution would be impossible and absurd: impossible because not all of the things we would want to count as resources on any reasonable view (cows, for instance) are physically capable of being divided up into n identical pieces; and absurd because an identical distribution takes no account of the varying needs, tastes, ambitions, etc. of the people making up the universe, so that almost everyone would end up with a very inconvenient bundle, with lots of useless items, but too little of what is really desired.

The obvious way forward is to substitute for identical bundles, bundles of equal value. This gets round both problems at once, for it avoids the problem of division by allowing people to make up a shortfall in one good by having more of another; and it avoids the individual variation problem by allowing individuals to have access to their preferred combination of goods, subject to the constraint that each has a bundle whose overall value is the same. But it lands us with a new problem, namely how to compute the value of a bundle of goods, once we allow that individual tastes etc. vary. For it will not then be any use asking Bill to decide whether bundle A and bundle B are of equal value, since all that he can reasonably decide is whether they are of equal value *to him*, and an affirmative answer by no means implies that they will also be of equal value to Tom and Jerry.

An ingenious attempt on this problem has been made by Ronald Dworkin in his paper 'Equality of Resources', where he presents a

---

practice of exchange, with all its remoter effects (see R. Nozick, *Anarchy, State and Utopia* (Oxford: Blackwell, 1974), esp. 160–4, 262–4). It would take us too far afield to expose the defects in Nozick's argument. My point here is that you can allow choice to have some significance without supposing, as libertarians do, that it must dominate all other considerations.

model for thinking about the problem of equal distribution in the form of a hypothetical auction. We are to imagine a society of people having to share out a finite set of items, which are divided into lots and then auctioned off, each person being provided with the same number of tokens with which to bid. The auction is run a number of times until each person is satisfied with the lots he has acquired, in the sense that he knows that there is no better set he could have acquired with his fixed number of tokens. At that equilibrium point the distribution of goods is 'envy-free', as economists would say, meaning that no-one prefers any one else's bundle to his own (if anyone *were* to be envious in this sense, they could ask for the auction to be run again and this time bid for the bundle they have spotted in someone else's possession). The price of each good in the auction will be a function of the quantity available and the aggregate demand, a resultant of each of the n individuals' valuation of that good against all the rest. Dworkin argues that this quasi-market method of establishing relative values (and hence defining equality of resources) is appropriate.

> The auction proposes . . . that the true measure of the social resources devoted to the life of one person is fixed by asking how important, in fact, that resource is for others. It insists that the cost, measured in that way, figure in each person's sense of what is rightly his and in each person's judgment of what life he should lead, given that command of justice.[14]

Suppose now we think of applying Dworkin's model to a real society, in the sense that we try to assign all the existing resources at any moment by using the auction device. What difficulties would we encounter? One difficulty is that not all of the things we would reasonably want to count as resources could successfully be put up to auction. Dworkin assumes that the items in the auction will be held as private property, used exclusively by the person who bids for them. But many features of our environment that contribute to welfare have to a greater or lesser degree the character of public goods, in the sense that they can only be provided for everyone or no-one—beautiful landscapes, for instance. Even if these were to be marked up as lots in the auction, no-one will bid for them at anything like full value, since nearly all of that value would spill over on to others. Hence their fate would be to be reconstituted into lots that would attract private bidders. This is, of course, simply the analogue of the fact that markets are not an effective way of channelling demand for public goods, since in general it will not be in anyone's interest to supply them, given the lack of private buyers. So

---

[14] R. Dworkin, 'Equality of Resources', *Philosophy and Public Affairs*, **10** (1981), 289.

the auction model seems not to achieve the neutrality that it promises as a conception of equality of resources, but rather confines the resources that will be counted in to those that would be bid for as private property.

One might reply to this by saying that we need to think up some other device to operate alongside the auction to deal with the public goods problem; one would then have a two-part notion of equality: equality of (private) resources *plus* equal access to public goods. Dworkin suggests something like this. But the problem here is that different people will place different relative values on goods of the two kinds, so to ensure equality in the total bundles of goods enjoyed by each person, we need a way of establishing the relative values of public and private goods—say of beautiful landscapes and motor cars—in the way that the Dworkinian auction establishes the relative values of different kinds of private commodities.

So my first comment on Dworkin's equality of resources model is that it arbitrarily confines the scope of resources to privately held items. A second difficulty with the model concerns its application over time. Suppose that a regime of equality of resources has been established at some moment and then consider the distribution as it alters over time. I shall ignore for the moment individual differences in talent and productivity, since I intend to deal with these shortly under the heading of internal resources. Consider simply what people may do with the resources they have been allocated. Patterns of use will vary according to personal taste and so forth. Some will consume their resources quickly, others will store theirs up, yet others will gamble, etc. Equality between the bundles will not persist, nor indeed should it, since the argument for equality of resources and against equality of welfare was that a distribution based on the latter principle would respond in an inappropriate way to personal choices. It seems quite acceptable that there should be welfare differences that reflect the fact of choice. Hence, even regardless of the practicalities, it would be wrong in principle to intervene to preserve equality of resources over time. The point of that conception of equality is to identify a starting point from which people will go on to lead their lives as they choose.[15]

But now consider various other factors that may, over time, alter the relative value of originally equivalent bundles of goods. One factor

[15] Dworkin attempts to distance his account from what he calls 'the starting-gate theory of fairness'. But he understands this as involving a Lockean theory of resource acquisition, and fails to notice that in a broader and more natural sense, his theory of equality of resources is also a starting-gate theory. For an analysis of this point, see G.A. Cohen, 'Self-Ownership, World-Ownership and Equality: Part II', *Social Philosophy and Policy*, **3** (1985–6), 77–96, section IV.

would be natural processes. Climatic changes, say, might alter the relative value of different parcels of land. Another factor would be discoveries. Since I am continuing for the moment to ignore questions of production, these would have to be discoveries about the consumption uses of goods—say that a certain plant was edible, or had medicinal properties. Once again, the effect would be to change the relative values of all bundles of goods, depending on how much of the good in question they contained. But I want to focus on a third factor, namely general changes of taste, which would again alter the relative desirability of different bundles of goods. Note that this must be kept distinct from the question of the effect that *my* changes of taste may have on *my* welfare. We have already said that, given my bundle of goods, if I choose to cultivate a taste for champagne and so have less welfare overall, that is my responsibility. But the problem now is one of a general shift from, say, beer-drinking to wine-drinking, which will enhance the value of all bundles of goods containing vineyards and depress the value of all bundles of goods containing hop-plantations. It will be difficult for an egalitarian to agree that *I* should lose out because of changes in *other people*'s tastes (supposing I own a hop-plantation). All of this is a simple reflection of the fact that equality of resources was defined through a process that unearthed the relative social values of different goods, while at the same time goods are valued not for their intrinsic features but for what they can do for us.

We find, then, that advocates of equality of resources are caught in a cleft stick. On the one hand, they want to establish an initial allocation of resources that is not sensitive to the choices made by each individual taken separately, since that would nullify responsibility for personal choice and collapse equality of resources into equality of welfare. On the other hand, given that the auction device values resources according to overall relative preferences for different kinds of goods, the initial equality must be upset whenever there is a general shift in taste. If, in order to cope with the second problem, it is proposed that the auction should be re-run at regular intervals, the upshot will be that the new distribution is sensitive to all changes of taste in the intervening period, and no one need be penalized for the new tastes they have chosen to develop during that time. Dworkin's aim that people should decide what sorts of lives to pursue within the constraints of a prior distribution of resources will be defeated. In short, you cannot both define equality of resources in a manner that is responsive to tastes and also treat equality as a mode of distribution that is not disturbed by individual choices.

A somewhat similar dilemma is posed by internal resources, that is personal capacities such as skills and talents. These are 'resources' in the sense that, like external goods, they can be deployed so as to enhance the welfare of their possessor. The question, then, is whether the equality of resources doctrine should be applied to them too, and if so how.

We may think that the doctrine does not apply at all in this case. People's skills and talents are integral parts of them, and they deserve the fruits of deploying those capacities on whatever share of external resources has justly been assigned to them. (This intuition is sometimes dressed up in the language of self-ownership.) Although I am sympathetic to this line of argument, I do not wish to pursue it here, since it seems a clear case of the principle of desert conflicting with and vanquishing the principle of equality. There is no reason to expect the outcome of a system in which external resources are equally distributed but people are allowed to enjoy the fruits of their talents to be strongly egalitarian.[16]

The alternative, therefore, is to find some way of distributing internal resources equally. Obviously this cannot be done literally, but the thought is that it might be possible to counterbalance inequalities of talent by giving additional external resources to the less talented. The proposal, then, is that we should aim for overall equality of resources, placing external and internal resources into a single pool. How might such a proposal be carried through?

One proposal is that talents should be auctioned off in the Dworkinian fashion along with everything else. That is, along with the cows and the chickens and so forth there would be a lot marked 'David Miller's talents', whose price in the auction would be determined by the general estimate of its usefulness. It is likely that each person would in the first place bid to secure ownership of their own talents, but the price paid would vary according to the estimate—so that those with valuable talents would have fewer tokens left with which to bid for their bundle of external resources. Leaving aside the slightly surreal quality of this scenario, what are the problems of principle it raises? The main one is that the talented are likely to end up worse off, in welfare terms, than the untalented. The price of a talent will be based on judgments about its maximally effective use, just as will judgments about a resource of any kind. Now it may well be that my tastes are such that I do not want to use my talent in this most effective way. I prefer to be a don, say, even though I could earn most as an accountant; and I will almost

---

[16] I am thinking here of a system which allows full private ownership of resources, including virtually unlimited contractual rights (this is what Dworkin intends). If constraints are placed on the uses to which people may put the resources allocated to them, the conclusion will have to be modified. See my discussion in *Market, State and Community* (Oxford: Clarendon Press, 1989), Ch. 6.

certainly want to have more leisure than my internal resources require for their reproduction. But the price I have had to pay takes no account of these personal preferences, so I end up with a package of external and internal resources that produces less well-being than will typically accrue to someone else who could buy himself more cheaply. John Roemer has put this point in an illuminating way: 'A highly talented person is exactly like a person with an involuntary expensive taste: the only kind of leisure he likes to consume is expensive leisure, his own. His leisure is expensive because it has an alternative use which is highly valued by society.'[17]

Roemer's formulation also highlights what is objectionable about the proposed mechanism for equalizing talents. Since we have already rejected equality of well-being as a goal, it might seem no objection to the present conception of equality of resources that the talented will end up worse off in terms of well-being. But the point is that talents are something you are landed with—normally of course an advantage to you, but under the regime we are considering a liability. The welfare differences that emerge reflect endowment, not choice. And this result can be generalized to other mechanisms that attempt to correct for inequalities of personal productive capacity—for instance a proportional tax on abilities.[18] The point again is that tax rates will be based on the predicted results of deploying your talents in the maximally productive way, and so will penalize people who decide to do something else with their lives.

So we seem again here to have two somewhat unattractive poles to choose between. Either we allow people to reap the full benefits of their personal capacities and end up with a society that is quite inegalitarian in its distribution of resources (and presumably of welfare too); or we attempt to correct for inequalities of talent and end up with what has been called with some hyperbole 'the slavery of the talented'—slavery to society because of their own productive potential. And here it may be tempting to look for some practical fudge, as Dworkin does when he proposes an income tax and transfer payments as a surrogate for the insurance he believe people would be willing to take out if they did not know how talented they would be.[19] Income taxes may partially redistribute the returns of ability; but of course they also impinge on choice. People are taxed for choosing to lead one sort of productive life (the financially lucrative sort) rather than another. There may be good practical reasons for raising revenue in this way, but it is hard to find a rationale for income taxation in terms of ideas of justice and equality.

[17] J. Roemer, 'Equality of Talent', *Economics and Philosophy*, **1** (1985), 165.
[18] See the general discussion in Roemer, 'Equality of Talent'.
[19] Dworkin, 'Equality of Resources', sections V–VI.

David Miller

I conclude, therefore, that there are serious difficulties with both parts of the equality of resources idea—both with equality of external resources and with equality of personal talents. Equality of resources does not seem to provide a viable alternative to equality of welfare, which we have already found to be open to damaging objections. Now, having come this far, it may be tempting to try to thread our way between these two unacceptable ideas of simple equality, searching for some formula that picks up what is defensible in each and discards what is indefensible. This is the motivation that lies behind such proposals as Arneson's *equality of opportunity for welfare* and Cohen's *equality of access to advantage*.[20] Yet although both authors make a good case for believing that their proposals are superior both to unmodified equality of welfare and to unmodified equality of resources, in neither case do we any longer have a simple idea of equality in the sense explained above. Cohen is quite explicit that his notion of 'advantage' rolls together two heterogeneous components, resources and welfare, and regrets that he has not yet found 'a currency more fundamental than either resources or welfare in which the various egalitarian responses which motivated my proposal can be expressed'.[21] But once equality is seen as a matter of *combining* separate dimensions to give an overall index, we have already crossed the border between simple and complex notions, and there seems no reason not to consider other dimensions beyond those canvassed by Arneson and Cohen.

III

Let us turn, then, to ideas of complex equality, whose defining feature is the claim that independent distributions along a number of separate dimensions may give rise to a condition of overall equality. Note

[20] R. Arneson, 'Equality and Equal Opportunity for Welfare', *Philosophical Studies*, **54** (1988), 79–95; G. A. Cohen, 'On the Currency of Egalitarian Justice', *Ethics*, **99** (1988–9), 906–44.

[21] Cohen, 'On the Currency of Egalitarian Justice', 921. In Arneson's case, the complexity is less apparent, but it can be brought out by considering the definition he offers of equal opportunity for welfare. 'For equal opportunity for welfare to obtain among a number of persons, each must face an array of options that is equivalent to every other person's in terms of the prospects for preference satisfaction it offers' ('Equality and Equal Opportunity for Welfare', 87). Should 'prospects for preference satisfaction' be assessed using each individual's own preferences, or using some standardized measure of preference satisfaction? If the former, how do we prevent expensive tastes from influencing the outcome? If the latter, how is the metric to be constructed given diversity of tastes among individuals?

straightaway that there are two possible ways of formulating this claim. One, which can be found in Bernard Williams' paper 'The Idea of Equality', portrays the distributions themselves as egalitarian. Williams identifies two main aspects of the idea of equality, equality of respect, which requires us to treat people as self-conscious agents with their own ways of understanding their situation (and not merely as occupants of externally-defined roles, for example); and equality of opportunity, which enjoins us to distribute scarce goods on morally relevant grounds (such as merit and need). These two requirements may in some cases pull apart, in which case, Williams tells us, 'we should not throw one set of claims out of the window; but should rather seek, in each situation, the best way of eating and having as much cake as possible.'[22] The picture here is of two forms of equality, each making powerful demands on us, and our task as one of trading off between them in such a way as to achieve the highest combined value of equality of respect and equality of opportunity.

In Michael Walzer's formulation, by contrast, there is no suggestion that each distribution taken by itself is egalitarian. Walzer portrays a condition of social pluralism in which there are many different kinds of goods, each carrying with it its own criterion of just distribution. Provided these criteria are adhered to, and each sphere of justice safeguarded from invasion by neighbouring spheres, complex equality can be achieved overall. But this does not require the criteria themselves to be egalitarian. Some of the goods identified by Walzer are indeed (properly) distributed equally—citizenship, to take only the clearest example; but most are not, and in the case of goods such as money, the thrust of his argument is that there should be no attempt to impose a patterned distribution at all.

I am not aiming here at a complete discussion of Walzer's theory of justice, but at the particular claim that pluralism as he describes it creates a condition of *equality*. How is this claim to be read? Walzer explains it as follows:

> In formal terms, complex equality means that no citizen's standing in one sphere or with regard to one social good can be undercut by his standing in some other sphere, with regard to some other good. Thus, citizen X may be chosen over citizen Y for political office, and then the two of them will be unequal in the sphere of politics. But they will not be unequal generally so long as X's office gives him no advantages over Y in any other sphere—superior medical care, access to better schools for his children, entrepreneurial opportunities, and so on.[23]

[22] Williams, 'The Idea of Equality', 131.
[23] M. Walzer, *Spheres of Justice* (Oxford: Martin Robertson, 1983), 19.

David Miller

Perhaps the most obvious way to read this passage is to see it as proposing a principle of compensation: citizen X may be ahead in the sphere of politics, but Y will be ahead in the sphere of money, Z in the sphere of Divine Grace, and so forth. No individual, or set of individuals, will enjoy superiority of goods along all dimensions, and equality results from balancing goods of one kind off against goods of other kinds. Y's relative disadvantage in the sphere of political office is compensated by his relative advantage in the sphere of money. This reading is supported by the passage immediately following the one I have quoted, where Walzer considers the possibility that the same people might succeed in every sphere. His reaction to this hypothesis is to say that no form of equality would then be on the cards.

On reflection, however, there are difficulties with the compensation reading of Walzer's equality claim. One immediate difficulty is that not all of the goods that Walzer cites are goods that people value in the way that the argument requires. Take medical care for instance. Although it is plainly a good thing to have medical care when you are sick, it is better still not to be sick in the first place, and it would be absurd to think of someone who receives an above-average quota of medical care as being compensated for his poor standing in the spheres of money or power. More fundamentally, one cannot run the compensation argument alongside the claim that social goods are constituted in such a way that they are fundamentally different in kind. For the latter claim implies incommensurability: if money and political power, say, are two radically different currencies, then no conversion between them will be possible. One cannot specify a cash equivalent for the value of holding office in local government, say. Assertions of that kind presuppose some way of translating quantities of power into quantities of money and vice versa. This runs directly counter to Walzer's underlying assumption that each of the goods he considers is *sui generis*. And if conversion is impossible, then the compensation argument breaks down. If Y is inferior to X in the sphere of political office, it makes no sense to think of this as being *compensated* by his monetary advantages. We could speak of equality *within* a particular sphere, but not of equality *across* spheres.

A second reading of Walzer's equality claim would focus on his opposition to dominance, which he defines as a state of affairs in which individuals possessing a certain good are able, by virtue of that fact alone, to command a wide range of other goods. Where complex equality obtains, in contrast, my success in obtaining any particular good—office let us say—will depend only on how I perform by the criteria relevant to that sphere; money, for instance, cannot be used to determine access to the office. This claim, I believe, is best interpreted as a claim about equality of power, in its broadest sense. Complex quality rules out the consolidation of inequalities of power, whereby advantage in one sphere can be converted into advantage in others.

Read in this way, however, Walzer's egalitarianism becomes very weak. Imagine a society in which there are a few very wealthy men, a few with great political power, a few with high reputations in intellectual life, and so on, but in which the vast majority of people have low scores on all these dimensions. Complex equality obtains insofar as the autonomy of the different spheres of achievement is respected. In what sense does this society embody equality of condition? My efforts to win political office are not blocked by the power of the wealthy (for instance), but they are fruitless none the less. The distributive mechanisms are such that someone with my very ordinary array of talents cannot achieve pre-eminence in any of the spheres of justice. Although no doubt preferable to what Walzer calls 'tyranny'—the dominance of one particular good and its holders—complex equality so understood seems unlikely to satisfy any egalitarian worth his salt.

I want to propose a third reading of Walzer's claim which is avowedly revisionist but which still, I hope, captures something of the spirit of the original. My proposal is that we should treat Walzer's claim as a claim about equality of *status*. Complex equality creates a state of affairs in which people regard and treat one another as of equal standing overall, despite the fact that in particular spheres achievements and holdings of goods are visibly unequal.

This proposal would pick up Tocqueville's idea which I referred to at the beginning of the paper. When Tocqueville talked about 'equality of condition', he did not mean economic or any other distributive form of equality, but equality in social life generally. The contrast was with hierarchy, embodied for him in the Ancien Régime, a state of affairs in which each person occupied a social position, and people looked up to or down on others according to their respective stations. Social equality, conversely, meant that people regarded one another as their peers, did not defer or condescend.

What conditions are necessary for equality of status to obtain? There seem to me to be two fundamental requirements. First, the public institutions of the society we are considering must treat all members as equals, in particular by extending equal rights of citizenship to all. These rights will include the equal protection of the laws, rights of political participation, and so forth. The point here is that equality of status must be inscribed and expressed in a society's public arrangements.[24] Second, other distributive arrangements must be so con-

---

[24] Walzer does of course recognize the importance of equal citizenship, but he does not perhaps stress sufficiently the central role it plays in the specification of an egalitarian society (though see his discussion of self-respect and self-

stituted that unequivocal judgments of higher and lower social standing cannot be made.

The first of these conditions seems relatively straightforward although we may expect a continuing debate on the question how far the rights of citizenship should extend (should they, for instance include certain rights to welfare?). The second condition is somewhat more problematic. It builds on Walzer's core idea that equality may result from differential performance in a variety of spheres. It does not however, require that there should be precise compensation across these spheres, a requirement that we earlier saw to be unsustainable once the diversity of goods is recognized. The condition is rather that performances should be sufficiently diverse that the public at large cannot make clear-cut judgments of unequal status. Bill may be better at making money than Tom, but Tom is a writer whose novels receive widespread acclaim, so we cannot rank them against each other overall. Here the incommensurability of goods can be seen to work in favour of equality rather than against it. In so far as Bill and Tom score along radically different dimensions, we cannot rank them comparatively and so their social status must rest simply on their common standing as citizens of this society.

So far the argument runs along Walzerian lines. Unlike Walzer however, I do not believe that separation of spheres is sufficient by itself to achieve the second condition for equality of status. We need also to say something about the extent of inequality within spheres especially the spheres of power and money. Where inequalities in these areas are very large, they can effectively swamp the other dimensions which in theory might serve to counteract them.[25] This seems plainly to be true of societies such as our own: they are societies in which although class boundaries are more fluid than they were in the past hierarchical class distinctions are still made, chiefly because vast ine

---

esteem in *Spheres of Justice*, 272–80, where the connection is made). For Walzer, the political sphere has a special status chiefly because it is the means whereby we can preserve (or achieve) the separation of the other spheres of justice. My focus here is upon the symbolic importance of citizenship as the sphere in which the equality (or inequality, as the case may be) of people belonging to different social categories is publicly declared.

[25] In saying this, I might seem to be conceding that the different goods are commensurable after all, contrary to my earlier argument. This is not what I intend. The point is rather that our judgments of social standing generally invoke multiple criteria. When several criteria are brought into play, incommensurability means that no overall ranking is possible. But sometimes one criterion, such as wealth, appears to us so overwhelmingly salient that no other yardsticks are considered. This is a claim about the psychology of social status not about the logic of assessment.

qualities of wealth translate into patterns of life that differ completely from one another. Because one form of differentiation is so salient, it cannot be offset in social judgment by performances in other spheres. And although Walzer would no doubt argue (with justification) that our societies are distorted by dominance, especially the dominance of money, this is not the whole answer. Even if the rich scrupulously prevented their wealth from influencing the distribution of goods of other sorts, we would still not have a society of equal status.

Unfortunately it does not seem possible to say in general terms what limits need to be placed on inequalities of wealth and power in order to secure equality of status. Tocqueville saw in America a country where, although considerable fortunes were made and lost, the wealthy never consolidated themselves into a separate class; he was struck by the easy intercourse between rich and poor. Since then, many other observers have contrasted the classless ethos of the new societies of North America and Australasia with the older European societies in which hierarchical class divisions still persist, despite the fact that the two groups of countries display broadly similar distributions of income and wealth.[26] This suggests that the conversion of money differences into inequalities of status is by no means a straightforward process, but depends rather on cultural factors unique to each society. At the same time there may be no doubt, in a particular case, that prevailing inequalities of wealth and power far exceed those compatible with equality of status, and the direction that public policy should take will be sufficiently clear.

I believe that the idea of equality of status best captures the egalitarian agenda of the present period. The ideas of simple equality examined in the last section—equality of welfare, equality of resources and their variants—find few supporters outside the ranks of academic political philosophy. Equality of status—the idea of a classless society, or, to put it more concretely, a society in which people outscore one another along particular dimensions but are not judged more or less worthy or successful overall—has a much wider resonance. I have argued that it is best understood as a form of complex equality. Equality of status does not mean that there is some characteristic, viz. status,

[26] There are, of course, some differences in distributive pattern within each group. My point is that the Old World does not systematically exhibit greater economic inequality than the New World. Estimates for the distribution of income only are given in H. Lydall, *The Structure of Earnings* (Oxford: Clarendon Press, 1968), Ch. 5. This picks out New Zealand and Australia as enjoying a particularly high degree of equality, but places Canada and the United States below the United Kingdom, West Germany and the Scandinavian countries in a middle group of moderately equal societies. France stands out among industrialized societies as exceptionally inegalitarian.

that is handed out in equal quantities to each person.[27] Rather there are many specific distributions which, when properly arranged, have the effect that no overall social rankings are possible, and so equality of status appears as a by-product. Michael Walzer's work has provided the inspiration for this argument, but I have interpreted his position in a particular way, and I am less sanguine than he is that keeping the spheres of justice separate is sufficient by itself to ensure equality of condition.

[27] Note, however, that in my account equality of status does require one simple form of equality, namely equal citizenship. This *is* properly construed as requiring an equal distribution (of rights, etc.) to everyone.

Equality
A Response

KENNETH MINOGUE

David Miller has provided for us a lucid and brilliant account of the rich theoretical literature which took off in the late sixties, and has been hardly at all affected by the dominance of market ideas and practices in the 1980s. Most people, I should guess, take for granted that something vaguely describably as 'a more equal society' is in itself a good thing. Even more, no doubt, believe that the problems of the 'Third World' result from the extreme inequalities common in those countries. Equality is, then a central issue both in politics and among some philosophers.

Miller goes further, and suggests, in Tocquevillian terms, that there is something providential in the egalitarian ferment which is seldom absent from modern states. He might well have cited Aristotle, who takes equality to be the passion at the heart of revolutions: '. . . inferiors become revolutionaries in order to be equals, and equals in order to be superiors.'[1] It was in part no doubt the experience of market relations which made the Greeks susceptible to the lure of egalitarianism, and Miller argues that market relations are inherently likely to generate an egalitarian ethos. The obvious paradox is that the market must, in doing so, begin to encompass its own destruction. This is a paradox little explored by egalitarians, for whom it is a vital presupposition that production is unaffected by legislative redistribution. But it is the paradox which anyone like myself would make the focus of attention. For it is characteristic both of the egalitarian on the Clapham omnibus, and of the philosophical egalitarian, that neither pays any attention to the agency—'in practice the state and its various branches,' as Miller nonchalantly puts it—which must organize and enforce this popular ideal. In the past, the main concomitant of egalitarian measures has been a social service ministry and a horde of civil redistributors. But as egalitarianism has spread into wider and wider spheres of social life, a new type of agency has come to be increasingly prominent: the tribunal. Egalitarianism is one lever by which the life of modern societies is progressively judicialized. The beneficiaries of redistribution become pensioners of the state; increasingly, they also become

[1] Aristotle, *Politics*, V ii.

claimants at a court. It seems to me obvious that a tendency of this kind must necessarily have long term consequences for the character of societies thus 'egalitarianized'.

Before moving to matters of substance, I must make it clear that in opposing egalitarianism, I am not arguing in favour of anti-egalitarianism. These are the options David Miller poses for us, but the second term seems to me crucially ambiguous.

Inequality is notoriously the common condition—one might well say 'the natural condition'—of mankind. An 'inegalitarian' as the opposite of an egalitarian would presumably be the partisan of some specific sort of inequality—one based on blood, for example. My disagreement with egalitarianism is thus both particular and general. I oppose not only the plan of equality, but any kind of plan at all. I take the state to be a specific type of association in which resourceful individuals recognize a sovereign power able to enforce the conditions of peace permitting the citizens to live their lives as they choose. To bend that power to the end of imposing any kind of abstract outcome, whether egalitarian or inegalitarian, seems to me something for which no serious reason could be given. Specific measures of redistribution—for the relief of poverty, for example—might well be publicly judged necessary, but any such measures both can and ought to be justified in specific terms, and not in terms of some overriding plan to be imposed on a whole society.

The study of equality, however, usually manages to get by in intellectual circles by occupying the high ground of a moral ideal. It barely raises a philosophical issue at all. It is, rather, a form of high level practical politics drawing upon many of the technicalities of recent theories of action, public choice, personal identity and so on. Not infrequently (as in the 'Dworkinian auction' Miller describes) it has all the look of science fiction carried on by other means. But egalitarianism is by no means without influence in the world, since it represents the justificatory armoury of a sect deeply entrenched in the bureaucracies of contemporary liberal-democratic states which, not greatly influential at the polls, none the less exerts great influence in the law courts, the central and local administrative systems, pedagogic institutions, and among the intelligentsia generally. Equality is, *par excellence*, the project of the social engineer, and the failure of such projects to commend themselves greatly to electorates may perhaps best be explained by the fact that engineering is more fun for the engineer than it is for the ordinary people who would be subjected (notionally for their own benefit) to this Procrustean exercise.[2]

___

[2] I refer here, of course, to an invigorating critique of the ideal of equality by the philosopher Antony Flew, in *The Politics of Procrustes* (London: Temple Smith, 1981).

It is worth invoking the metaphor of engineering because it immediately brings to the surface the unreality which, as we have noted, characterizes the entire theoretical literature on equality—a literature which, I repeat, is at best on the very margins of philosophy. The unreality is the remarkable absence of attention paid to the agency which will bring this goal about. We know perfectly well that this agency will have to be quite remarkable because virtually all the societies known to us have been characterized by many complex forms of inequality. It must thus be capable of nothing less than a transformation of human nature. Yet Miller pays no attention whatever to this problem, and in doing so, he is entirely representative of the literature he is describing. It is enough to turn one into a deconstructionist, this averting of the eyes from the question of agency. It makes one look with increasing interest at the silences of the genre. There is, for example, a great recourse to the passive voice. There is also a certain concealment behind the opacities of the plural first person pronoun: 'If equality of welfare is a way of showing equal concern for each person, then we do that by providing the appropriate share of resources in the first place . . .', we read[3] and the 'we' in question is clearly not the philosophical 'we' linked by joint agreement on some stage of an argument, but a practical distributor disposing of resources in the world. But of 'ways of showing equal concern for persons' there is in fact no end: those brutal sergeants in war movies licking rookies into shape were doing that. No necessary connection links a motive to an act. I cite this point because it illustrates the way in which questions in the philosophy of action are taken for granted in pursuit of what are not really philosophical questions at all. But, returning to my quest for any concern with the agency which will bring the goal of equality about, let me cite the one moment where this vital term of the relationship between goal and implementation does actually surface: In order to take seriously the idea of equality of well being (an idea soon in Miller's paper to be superseded) 'some agency—in practice the state and its various branches—would need to gather information about each person's welfare function in order to establish what assignment of rights, etc. would implement equality of well-being'.[4]

Now a state which did such a thing, indeed, a state which could *possibly* do such a thing, would be a very remarkable institution indeed, and the appropriate philosophical reflex would be to turn round to consider what such an institution might be. Given the sheer volatility of human welfare functions, one might easily conclude that such a thing would be, not only unbearably intrusive, but barely conceivable. If so,

[3] Miller, see above, 85.
[4] Miller, see above, 84.

we have, in egalitarian theory, the interesting spectacle of a great deal of thought being given to a practical project which is actually impossible, and indeed could be seen to be impossible on the most casual inspection. I am not at all inclined simply to say: 'that way madness lies', because I believe that the real significance of the passion for equality lies quite elsewhere. But it is worth observing that we are not, in opening up the occluded question of the equalizing agent, operating in a field without empirical confirmation. It is of the essence of communism to bring about an egalitarian society, and revolutionary social engineers have got to work on a variety of societies in the twentieth century intending to bring about equality. They have, in fact, taken a minimal interest in the welfare functions of their subjects, rather demanding that these functions should adjust to what the social engineers take to be the ideal social order. As everyone knows, these versions of egalitarianism have had horrific consequences. It is but one more of the significant silences of egalitarian literature that any mention of these events is treated as in vulgar bad taste. No one, by invoking Stalin, Mao, Pol Pot, etc., would want to suggest that the theoretical egalitarians who have produced the literature we are considering have the slightest inclination towards exercising this kind of despotic power over their fellow citizens. Still, major questions about egalitarianism are raised by these undoubtedly egalitarian experiences, and regularly ignored by the philosophers of this ambitious project of making everybody equal.

Egalitarian theory, then (I prefer not to call it philosophy), is marked by a defensive concern with the locutionary content of a range of implications of the project, and a great reluctance to look to left or right, not only at the real world in which the goal would have to be pursued, but also a variety of genuinely interesting philosophical questions. One of these is the character of human life, and we may move to consider it by looking at the egalitarian taste for using the passive voice. What must be the nature of these creatures to whom 'are allocated' those equal shares in whatever happens to be the current focus of attention—well-being, resources, property, income, esteem, etc. to which may be added a great number of menacing additions, such as physical organs, the attention in conversation of their fellows, sexual attentions,[5] etc. The answer must be, I think, that these human beings must be construed simply as organisms in search of satisfaction, and that the goal of the egalitarian is to ensure that each such individual enjoys some

---

[5] I do not have space to exemplify the immense variety of things which one egalitarian or another thinks might be candidates for equalization but I have mentioned some of them in *The Egalitarian Conceit*, Centre for Policy Studies (London, 1989).

quantum of satisfactions equivalent to that of other individuals. It could only be some such passive creatures who might be imagined tamely to submit to this remarkable distributive agency which consults their welfare functions and allocates the goodies to them. Such a creature must also be imagined sufficiently docile and biddable to have no inclination to upset the egalitarian system either by acquisitive behaviour, or else by political agitation to change an egalitarian system which, being always conceived as a fixed terminus of political endeavour, must be forever changeless.

It is easy to understand how the egalitarian has come by such an account of the human condition, for it arises from the fact that the condition of inequality which the egalitarian seeks to remedy is in fact the running together of two quite separate conditions: that of the rich, and that of the poor. Now it is perfectly true that moralists have often found the rich 'a problem' on some such ground as that they lead wasteful and luxurious lives, but such puritanism is hardly plausible today, when the luxuries of the past have become the commonplaces of today. The rich are no doubt a focus of envy and hatred, and they challenge the homogenizations dreamed of by sea-greens incorruptible, but whatever we may say about them, they are not a 'problem' in the same sense as the poor may be thought a problem. We take the poor to be a problem because they suffer deprivation, and our contemporary sensibility recognizes a duty to prevent such suffering. But that duty has nothing whatever to do with redistributing the property of the rich. The basis of egalitarianism, then, is its yoking together of two quite separate questions—helping the poor, and dispossessing the rich—and this, in my view, is the muddle which accounts for much of the unthinking support which 'a more equal society' still has.

The egalitarian conception of man arises then pretty obviously from meditation upon the condition of the poor. It comes out even more clearly in the locutions commonly used in the technical literature of egalitarianism: the *de*prived, the *dis*advantaged, the *under*privileged, and so on. The conception is of people suffering from lack of material resources, education and other conditions commonly thought of, abstractly, as 'advantages'. The egalitarian project thus envisages active helpers of sad and pathetic sufferers. And this real root of the project cannot help but colour its entire development. It is the fantasy of succouring a helpless population prepared merely to be the recipients of equal shares in some set of goods.[6] What we have to consider, then, is, both in theory and in practice, a form of despotism, even if in the theoretical literature, it is a despotism mitigated by suburban values.

[6] Some moral theorists, such as Professor David Raphael, even invented a whole class of such rights for people, called 'rights of recipience'.

There is, of course, another quite different conception of the human condition found in Western thought, and to consider it will help us to understand the real significance in our civilization of the idea of equality. This conception is of human life as a challenge to self-exploration, an adventure in which both our triumphs and our failures contributte to self-understanding. This is a conception which finds room for gamblers, risk-takers, and those whose passion it is precisely to excel, i.e. *not* to be equal to others—all of these being people who could not be accommodated in an egalitarian society. It is above all true of such people that they find inequalities challenging, and an egalitarian society precisely does away with their *raison d'être*.[7] In saying this, we must move to the more general point: that any human society contains a wide variety of personalities, characters and temperaments, and that the social arrangements which suit some will not suit others. Some no doubt would find their fulfilment in an egalitarian society, others would find it the most intolerable form of boredom and domination. But the very problem from which political philosophy begins is, precisely, to discover what are the possible civil conditions which can accommodate this variety of temperaments (and genders) with the minimum likelihood of frustration. Egalitarianism ignores this problem, and advances as the solution to the problem of different ways of life the domination of one preferred form. We might even suggest that it is this intellectual error which explains the fact that actual attempts to create an egalitarian society have invariably produced slaughter, imprisonment and repression on a massive scale. It is only by disposing of the mavericks that the egalitarian engineer will have decently tractable material on which to work.

The historical roots of the actual equality we enjoy (by contrast with the equality projected by egalitarians) lie in the Greek *agora*, in Roman law, the Christian theology of the early centuries of our era, the practices of the barbarian tribes who overran the Empire, and a number of subsequent developments including the growth of universities and the Protestant reformation. This is much too complex a story even to be broached in a short compass, but there is one elementary point which deserves emphasis. The Greek conception of man distinguished humanity in terms of a capacity to lead the good life, which might be enjoyed either in its political or its philosophical forms. Such a Greek conception of citizenship continues to exert a powerful fascination over

[7] This is the source of one of the more interesting forms of self-contradiction with which egalitarianism is riddled. Among those who find the point of their lives in 'struggling against' inequalities are the egalitarians themselves. As Marx presciently noted, there would be no place for *him* in a communist society.

the minds of egalitarians, especially in their propensity to misappropriate Aristotle in their cause. The Greeks are indeed admirable, but it is necessary to remember that being human was, for them, a relative matter determined by participation in an ideal. This ideal rendered women, slaves, most foreigners and many Greeks inferior copies of the human model, and therefore incapable of being fully human. The philosophical view prevalent among the Greeks was of the kind we might now call 'elitist'. The source of wisdom was the knowledge found only among a few philosophers. Our Christian civilization, however, has created a more individualistic view of human life, in which the essence of the soul lies in the variable dispositions of human beings, and no single pattern of the good life can claim to be rational or authoritative. Egalitarianism is, in fact, a revival of this ancient Greek belief that there is an ideal pattern of life to which all human beings ought to conform.

In denying this view, however, our civilization has worked out forms of equality which play a real and vital part in our traditions of behaviour. The first we might mention is the Christian belief in an immortal soul. This is basic because it has ramified into our contemporary view that personal and domestic experiences are the basic source of social and political values—a reversal of the Greek view that the higher values were only to be found in public life. It is out of this fundamental idea that the whole terminology of modern rights emerges. At other times and places, personal satisfactions were entirely subordinated to the functioning of some all-embracing communal order.

The second basic equality is that before the law. Here is where we may discover our conception of justice, and it is the key to the character of the modern European state. This is a dynamic idea in European history, and we may observe over the centuries the process by which it dissolved the remnants of feudal privilege. Further, it defines by exclusion what is in our civilization found the most intolerable of all situations: the dominance of a master, or a despot. Now what characterizes a despot is that he is untrammelled by law, and may interfere in the particulars of the lives of those he dominates. Those who dream idealistic dreams of improving the lives of their fellow men have always been fascinated by the image of power opened up by despotism, and have been encouraged in such dreams by the simple fact that a law, in the sense in which we talk of the 'rule of law', is not a suitable instrument for social engineering. The problem is that the populations of Western states consider a law not as an instruction to behave in a certain way, but as another condition which they must take into account in pursuing *their* projects (and not the goals of the social engineer). There is thus a direct contradiction between the actual equality before the law which we currently enjoy, and that 'goal of equality' which agitates the egalitarian. Some egalitarians, of course, fantasise that something called 'education' can dissolve this contradiction by persuading people to change their attitudes, but since this device has failed in countries like the Soviet Union, in which it has had the benefit of three generations of application backed up by as much force as necessary, we may judge it unlikely to have much effect upon our sceptical and active populations.

There is a third form of equality which seems to me also to be of vital importance: equality of manners. It is unique to the West, and basic to how we carry on. It rests upon a dislike of prostration and a taste for dealing with equal and independent people. It not only accommodates but actually feeds off inequalities of wealth, status, rank, intelligence, beauty, etc. and issues in forms of equal consideration which can be seen in our everyday behaviour. It allows for the ceaseless reversals of role-playing, in which the waiter here is the patron there, and allows sometimes sardonic reversals, as in the old song: 'I've got my sergeant major working for me now.' No doubt there are officeholders and millionaires who can count on a certain amount of servility from their associates, but this is a character defect, a lack of courage and self-respect (often self-defeating) against which the social engineers of the world are in any case helpless. It is obviously only the servile of the present world who complain about all kinds of obscure power being exercised over people, and of the need to 'empower' the powerless so that they can take charge of their own lives. The significant thing is that those to be 'empowered' are understood to be passive and victimized—a conception which alerts us to the dread presence of the social engineer.

I have rehearsed these various forms of equality not merely because the understanding of them is indispensible to the philosophy of the state (and much of the work of Hobbes, Rousseau and Hegel, for example, is taken up with discussing them), but to make a distinction in the role concepts play in social and political understanding. These forms of equality are the *presuppositions* of our way of life. When we are enjoying the company of friends, we are not in the least concerned with the fact that equality is a presupposition of the relationship we call 'friendship' any more than when we ask 'What is the time?' we concern ourselves with the presuppositional question: 'What is time?' I take it that the real business of philosophy is to elicit and explore these presuppositions because it is only if we have thought deeply about them that we can untangle the muddles that often arise in political argument. Sometimes such concepts appear to us in the form of ideals. The term 'ideal' however is ambiguous. It may simply be a synonym for 'conceptual'; alternatively, it may refer to an abstract goal thought to be morally desirable. A concern with the ideal in the first sense is clearly a philosophical enterprise, but the second sense of ideal merely takes us into the never-never land of utopia. This confusion is rooted deep in our tradition of political thought, and finds its most famous illustration in Plato's *Republic*, which has been taken as 'ideal' in both senses of the word.

The goal of equality considered by David Miller and the writers whose work he discusses is clearly not the equality which is, as we have seen, a presupposition of our civil life. It is, rather, the kind of ideal which is, in all senses of the word 'utopian'. And a legitimate response to the proposal of a utopia, quite apart from its distance from reality, is to say that one does not find it desirable. Certainly I find the utopia of equality repellant, and I think that my reasons for doing so bear upon the philosophical issues. Equality is, in fact, the conceptual finery worn by the practice of the ration book, and as Lenin pointed out, those who control a rationing system have more power over a population than the priests of old who threatened hellfire. Egalitarianism appeals genuinely to idealists, but it also tempts those who are crazed with the lust for power, not to mention an assortment of lunatics, who may be comprehensively exemplified by the proposal, made when egalitarianism was fresh and young, in the French revolution, that church belfrys should be demolished as offending against the principle of equality.[8] Lunatics of this sort are, of course, indignantly repudiated by egalitarian theorists. Such people constitute another of those forbidden areas, like the history of twentieth-century communism, which (it is delicately insinuated) would only be invoked by unscrupulous polemicists who cannot keep their minds on fine and noble things. But the history of human folly has taught us that once a general principle has gained a foothold, there is no controlling the implications which may be drawn from it. Now equality is a principle of so abstract and exiguous a character as to contain absolutely any content that may occur to a febrile imagination. *Anything* at all might be equalized and I know of no principle by which egalitarians can block off what we should now regard as the more lunatic implications of this very thin, but awfully powerful, principle.

The object of our criticism must thus be not this or that form of equality proposed, but the whole principle of egalitarianism. And the reason that seems to me best for disposing of it is to consider how presumptuous it is to purport to lay down some fixed substantive condition of human life to which everybody else, including all future generations, must conform. It betokens an arrogance which quite takes my breath away. And in saying this, I am approaching another of the

---

[8] Christopher Hibbert, *The French Revolution* (Harmondsworth: Penguin, 1980), 247.

logical characteristics of egalitarianism. Let us broach it by asking: What is the opposite of egalitarianism?

The obvious answer would be to say: inegalitarianism. We need to distinguish, of course, between what is sometimes called the 'philosophical' opposite of a concept (i.e. non-egalitarianism) and the 'popular' opposite. But in this case, there do correspond to the popular opposite various doctrines which have had a not insignificant following. Some have believed that the aristocracy (hereditary or natural) ought to rule; others, the white race; still others, those who have merit, or have expert scientific knowledge. It well illustrates the slipperiness of the field we are considering that there is a certain asymmetry even between these two groups of ideas. Egalitarianism describes support for a certain *order* of things, whereas these inegalitarian doctrines would seem to identify the *class of person* who ought to determine the order of things. But is this contrast real? Do not both doctrines specify both the order, and the orderer? The real point is that both egalitarians *and* inegalitarians make a claim to superior knowledge about how a society ought to be constituted, and, significantly, in both cases, belief in the doctrine is an essential condition for the successful working of the order proposed. It would be intolerable to have an egalitarian society in which the population did not believe in the ideal of equality—such a situation could not possibly last. The real meaning of egalitarianism, the illocutionary force of its utterance, then, is that it is a claim to superior knowledge about the proper constitution of a human society. We thus arrive at the definitive contradiction at the heart of egalitarianism: it is a doctrine which *constitutes* an elite claiming power over the rest of society. Communists who have set up vanguard parties and tried to form anew the minds and habits of their fellows are thus not eccentric to the tradition of egalitarianism: they are merely following out precisely what is implicit in the very logic of the idea.

Egalitarianism *and* inegalitarianism are thus part of a family of political doctrines which seek to impose some substantive pattern upon modern societies. But in the modern world, technology and variable sensibilities produce such constant changes that it is impossible to specify in advance any necessary substantive forms of human life. The essential characteristic of the adventure of modernity is that we have launched ourselves into an unpredictable future. In egalitarianism, we find the most powerful contemporary expression of that yearning for a fixed natural order within which human beings have lived for many millennia. I do not myself think that there is any chance that we actually can go back. And I do not think I am alone in being glad that this is so.

Libertarianism: some conceptual problems

NORMAN BARRY

I

Perhaps the most remarkable event in social thought of the last twenty years has been the resurgence of various strands of individualism as political doctrines. The term 'individualism' is a kind of general rubric that encompasses elements of nineteenth century classical liberalism, *laissez-faire* economics, the theory of the minimal state, and an extreme mutation out of this intellectual gene pool, anarcho-capitalism. The term libertarianism itself is applied indiscriminately to all of those doctrines. It has no precise meaning, except that in a general sort of way libertarianism describes a more rigorous commitment to moral and economic individualism and a more ideological approach to social affairs than conventional liberalism. I suspect that its current usage largely reflects the fact that the word with the better historical pedigree, liberalism, has been associated, in America especially, with economic doctrines that are alien to the individualist tradition.

It has received little philosophical analysis. Outside specialist fields it is simply associated with *laissez-faire* economics, private property and the market and whatever rationale it has is utilitarian, or at least consequentialist, in kind. Indeed surprisingly, many of its most articulate proponents, e.g. Ludwig von Mises, Milton Friedman and, to a lesser extent Friedrich von Hayek[1], are avowed subjectivists and non-cognitivist in ethics and political philosophy. Curiously, when writers such as those make evaluative judgments they almost invariably take an 'aggregate' form, i.e. institutions such as the free market, private property, the rule of law are appraised favourably because they make 'society', or some present and future unknown people, better off.

I say surprisingly because those writers are eager to condemn more overt aggregationists, e.g. Benthamite utilitarians, for making collec-

[1] While not a subjectivist in his ethics Hayek clearly does not think, following Hume, that reason is capable of formulating an objective set of moral principles. Instead he argues that a process of evolution will select out those moral rules most conducive to prosperity and progress. See his *The Fatal Conceit* (London: Routledge, 1988).

tive welfare judgments that depend on the measurability and inter-personal comparability of utilities, some way of showing how the pains of some may be outweighed by the pleasures of others in the con-struction of a social utility function. It is important to note why the redistribution implied in Benthamite utilitarianism is objectionable to those contemporary economic liberals who make subtly not dissimilar aggregative judgments. While the 'harm' that accrues to some individ-uals through coercive redistribution is regretted that regret seems not to depend upon a theory of the inviolability of the individual (least of all his rights): judgments of this kind are thought to be private, subjective and incommunicable. Coercive redistribution is objected to because of its misallocative effects, its attempted sundering of those uniform laws of production and distribution that are central to neo-classical econom-ics and the operation of which make economic society more efficient.

Libertarianism begins to emerge as an autonomous social theory when individualism, and especially a theory of rights, is given a founda-tion independently of consequentialism, or which is at least an essential supplement to it. The deficiencies of crude consequentialism are obvious. To take one problem: entitlement to goods and resources. It may seem intuitively plausible that individuals should have a legitimate claim on property acquired through voluntary exchange but it is a logical truth that a market process must *begin* with objects that are not the product of exchange. Their possession cannot be justified on purely utilitarian grounds. Again, the entitlement to scarce and non-augmen-table resources, e.g. land which yields a 'rental' income to the lucky owner, has always been a problem for the market philosophers. But this is scarcely considered by consequentialists, who are almost exclusively concerned with the efficiency properties of free exchange.

There is a whole range of familiar moral problems that are also not considered by quasi-positivist economic liberals. This covers not merely claims to property and the nature and value of individuality but also the whole structure of rules and institutions which constitute the necessary conditions for any exchange to take place at all. Over-shadowing all these issues is the problem of the legitimate role of the state.

II

The fundamental claim of libertarian social theory is a moral one: it is that the only intrinsically valuable things are the experiences of individ-uals. There are no objective states of affairs that can be understood or appraised independently of the effect that they have individual atti-tudes, feelings and emotions. A common culture, an artistic tradition or a traditional way of life have no intrinsic value, though each may have considerable instrumental value in promoting that which is of intrinsic value, individual experiences. One normative pay-off, claimed by libertarians, from this individualism is that it puts a prohibition on the using of particular individuals, their property or their person, for an alleged collective good, a good that exists independently of more or less immediate desires. Nozick writes:

> there is no *social entity* with a good that undergoes some sacrifice for its own good. There are only individual people, with their own individual lives. Using one of these people for the benefit of others, uses him and benefits the others.[2]

This rejection of the idea that there are intrinsically valuable collective goods does not put a prohibition on the supply of *public* goods; goods such as clean air, defence, law and order etc. which for technical reasons cannot be priced by the market. For the libertarian their rationale is entirely a function of individual desiring: and desires may be expressed through a public mechanism, such as voting, as well as through the market. Public institutions are then no more than conduits for the efficient transmission of desires. It should be noted also that this rejection of the claim that there is intrinsic value in collective goods is not a crude knock-down rejection of, say, state aid to the arts. This could emerge from a legitimate voting procedure (which, incidentally, is always stricter than majority rule for libertarians) but its existence (and any other attributes of a common culture) is a function of individuals wanting it and not of its intrinsic desirability.

This individualism is designed to exclude autonomy being realised through collective institutions, ways of life etc. Freedom, for a libertarian, is not defined exhaustively in negative terms as merely the absence of restraint: for this simple definition tells us nothing of the value of liberty or indeed about the criteria for its legitimate limitation. Free action is autonomous action:[3] action that is not coerced or caused in some way and that is not the product of another person's will. It is not mere 'choice', since a person subject to overwhelming threats technically chooses. Freedom as autonomy requires that choices to be effective must be made from as wide a range as possible. It is here that the market becomes contingently necessary for the exercise of freedom as autonomy. It is justified not because it maximizes some aggregate welfare function but because it permits individuals to pursue their values.

[2] *Anarchy, State and Utopia* (New York: Basic Books, 1974), 32–3.
[3] For a discussion of autonomy, see J. Griffin, *Well Being* (Oxford: Clarendon Press, 1986), Ch. xi. Also, J. Raz, *The Morality of Freedom* (Oxford: Clarendon Press, 1986), Chs. 14 and 15.

What is especially controversial in all this is the *a priori* assumption that freedom as autonomy is only reduced by coercion, i.e. by the state. The libertarian's major moral claim is that autonomy cannot be realized through collective action, aside from the supply of necessary public goods, since this entails the imposition of values on individuals. Yet it is surely conceivable that autonomy in the individualist's sense may be reduced non-coercively, i.e. by the market. The apparently random distribution of initial resources (which, as I have pointed out, cannot be validated by the exchange model), the unpredictable course of economic fortune, the emergence of natural monopoly, may singly or in combination reduce the range of an individual's choices, and hence his autonomy, as effectively as coercion. Is it not the case that a person choosing between low wages and destitution is *caused* to act as he does?

Almost all libertarians concede that there is such a phenomenon as market power. The usual examples are the single supplier of water in a desert community and that power potentially exercisable by a doctor in a medical emergency. In neither case is coercion exercised yet individual autonomy is clearly reduced in such circumstances. Are not such examples infinitely extendable? If the libertarian's defence of the market were to rest on its autonomy-enhancing features alone anything short of a perfectly competitive market could well license state intervention.

Apart from the quasi-utilitarian, and not decisive argument, that such phenomena are less likely to occur under the market precisely because of its capacity to co-ordinate dispersed knowledge,[4] the second line of defence concerns the libertarian's understanding of the nature of responsibility and the attribution of blame. Unpleasant outcomes of spontaneous exchanges between individuals are not intended by any one person; to the extent that they occur they are the unpredictable consequences of the interactions of many unknown individuals. Just as value is indissolubly bound up with individual experiences so is moral blame. Whatever distress-alleviating actions were to be taken by the state they would have to be justified on other grounds than the advancement of personal autonomy since collective action can only do this in the supply of genuine public goods.

It follows from this individualistic postulate that whatever role the state has it must be neutral between the variety of ends, purposes and values that agents may wish to pursue. This persistent anti-perfec-

---

[4] For a standard account of the market's co-ordinating properties, see 1. Kirzner, *Competition and Entrepreneurship* (University of Chicago Press, 1973). The market as a co-ordinating mechanism should be distinguished from perfectly competitive equilibrium, see N. P. Barry, *The Invisible Hand in Economics and Politics* (London: Institute of Economic Affairs, 1988).

tionism proceeds from at least two interconnected sources within libertarian thought: one that stresses the ultimate unknowability of ideal forms of life and the other that proclaims inviolable rights as boundaries or barriers which the state ought not to cross. Anti-perfectionism has an undoubted intuitive appeal since the pursuit of intrinsically desirable ends by the state seems to involve the imposition of the good on individuals.

It is clear that this anti-perfectionism helps us to distinguish between libertarianism and historical liberalism, especially the type espoused by John Stuart Mill. For he does understand liberalism as a way of life whose goods—liberty of expression, tolerance, the pursuit of the 'higher pleasures' and so on—are intrinsically valuable. Within the intricacies and contradictions of Mill's thought there is a conception of the 'good life', a certain kind of progressive utility, which is valuable irrespective of individual desires.[5] What is insoluble in Mill's thought is how this aggregative criterion is to be constructed out of the variety of preferences in a free society, or indeed be made consistent with the more strictly libertarian parts of *On Liberty*. I mean here the principle that state action is only morally permissible when the interests of a person are harmed by the actions of another.

In contrast, the inherent subjectivism of libertarianism compels silence as to the goods that individuals may pursue and the particular outcomes that occur from interaction within the rules and processes of a free society. These often do not resemble in any recognizable way Mill's ideal of a liberal society: indeed, an unthinking obeisance to custom and convention, a mindless pursuit of consumerism and a distaste for rational enquiry are just as likely to occur. It should also be pointed out that libertarian neutrality is not necessarily the same as *pluralism*, the ideal that the good society is characterized by competing ends and purposes with none having a higher priority over any other. A neutral state does not have the duty to encourage such a society merely because it is not a necessary outcome of the interaction of desiring individuals. There is an analogy here with the argument that competitive processes may produce spontaneously outcomes which are not competitive but monopolistic. Can the libertarian remain neutral? Can he have no values?

More pertinently, it is suggested that libertarian neutrality is itself an impossible *ideal*. For surely, the state cannot be neutral between the

---

[5] Nevertheless, what is valuable must presumably be desired by somebody. The perfectionist argument is that value ought not to be equated with the satisfaction of *immediate* desires and, further, that objects of desire ought not to be considered equally valuable.

law-abider and the criminal? It cannot be indifferent to rape.[6] This criticism seems to me to be misguided, for although the libertarian does not have a theory of value he does have a theory of institutions and constraints. More than anything else, libertarianism is a theory about the institutional frameworks within which individuals pursue their subjective ends and these institutional frameworks provide the necessary constraints. Such constraints have a rationale independently of questions of the good.

One further point must be made in connection with political neutrality. It is true that liberal neutrality has been espoused in the context of egalitarianism (albeit of a muted kind). Thus writers such as Rawls and Dworkin[7] maintain a neutrality about ends but also authorize redistributive activity by the state. The argument takes roughly the form that for the state to remain silent in the face of extensive inequality would be to favour implicitly the advantaged over the disadvantaged; and hence not be properly neutral between persons. Where libertarianism differs from this view is its rigorous theory of *ownership*. While both individualisms condemn the use of coercion to maintain ideal forms of life, libertarianism objects to redistribution of 'rightfully' owned resources because it uses the interests of some on behalf of others.

It should be noted in passing that the redistribution implied in the non-libertarian theory of value-neutrality would have to be of initial resources, cash, land, inheritance, rather than the subsidization or zero price provision of certain consumption goods and services; for a redistribution of the latter kind would imply that some activities were intrinsically more desirable than others. This is a perfectionist judgment. It would follow then that the differences between the two forms of value-neutrality individualism, liberalism and libertarianism, are not as great as is sometimes supposed, for unless a decisive claim to ownership of initial resources can be established there is no necessary inconsistency between a redistribution of such resources and allowing market exchange to proceed unimpeded from that point. Indeed, some liber-

---

[6] See Raz, *The Morality of Freedom*, 114–17, for a valuable discussion of this point. A large part of this section has been very much influenced by Raz's excellent book.

[7] J. Rawls, *A Theory of Justice* (Oxford: Clarendon Press, 1972), 310–15 and R. Dworkin, 'Equality of Resources', *Philosophy and Public Affairs*, **10** (1981), 283–345. The liberal egalitarianism of both Rawls and Dworkin seems to derive from the view that unequal earnings that emerge from exercise of natural talents constitute a form of 'rental', or unearned income, to which the recipient has no moral entitlement.

tarians have recommended just this.[8] The point is that the economic theory of the market is not a theory of ownership: it is a theory of efficiency with only a minimal normative content (confined mainly to its autonomy-enhancing properties).

The major problem for the libertarian is to explain how such an attenuated view of the self could generate those social institutions which he concedes are essential for the functioning of an individualistic order. If collective institutions have no intrinsic value but are merely conduits for the transmission of private choices then it is hard to see how they could be other than conveniences, to be discarded (or reconstructed) according to choice. The moral aim of libertarianism, i.e. to reduce coercion to the minimum necessary to secure order and predictability, precludes those minor interventions the rationale of which lies in the preservation of an intrinsically valuable cultural inheritance. The rigorous anti-perfectionism of libertarianism, and its concomitant commitment to the *prima facie* equal validity of individual desires, would, claims Joseph Raz, 'undermine the chances of survival of many cherished aspects of our culture'.[9] It could be argued that it would do more than this, for if it made the validity of a political regime turn exclusively on subjective desire how could a Hobbesian authoritarian state be distinguished from a liberal order?

Yet the major claim of classical liberalism and libertarianism is that a social order is conceivable, practicable and morally justifiable (whether in an indirect utilitarian or in a rights sense is not germane to this issue) in the absence of a common culture or an over-riding purpose. The very genius of liberal-individualist theory is said to be exhibited in its explanation of how *anonymous* individuals, held together only by abstract rules and largely ignorant of each other's ends and purposes, nevertheless generate a complex, predictable and highly efficient order. It is what is meant by Hayek's Great Society, Popper's Open Society and more controversially, Michael Oakeshott's civil association;[10] though this last is expressed in an appropriately mystical way. Though none of these could be described as libertarian in any substantive sense, their anti-communitarianism and rejection of the need for over-riding purposes for social stability, accords with at least one of the explanatory postulates of the more extreme individualistic theories. What is crucial to the argument is a distinction between the notion of a common culture and that of common rules.

[8] See, for example, H. C. Simons, *Economic Policy for a Free Society* (University of Chicago Press, 1948).

[9] Raz, *The Morality of Freedom*, 162.

[10] See M. Oakeshott, 'The Character of a Modern European State', in *On Human Conduct* (Oxford University Press, 1975), 185–326.

The classical liberal and libertarian claim is that the concept of a common culture is inherently disputable and contested and that the consequent lack of agreement about its meaning has the strong implication that it cannot function as a solvent to typical moral and economic resource problems of a modern society. However, this does not imply that there cannot be agreement about rules which are sufficiently abstract to accommodate peacefully a variety of ultimately subjective ends. This is not to deny that the agreement of individuals to live by common rules is something of a cultural achievement; hence the element of relativism that is embedded in all but the most rationalistic 'natural rights' individualist doctrines. But it is to challenge the claim that there is a common culture, which is a source of intrinsic value independent of subjective choice.

III

The theoretical issue is whether it is possible to explain typical social institutions, rules, law, a constitution, the state and so on in terms of individual, subjective evaluations, or whether they defy such a dissolution. This has important normative implications because if it is true, it implies that the libertarian appraisal of government policy and the evaluation of existing institutions depends on how they meet with this individualistic criterion. The libertarian has to show that the collective goods espoused by communitarians as a source of value are no more than cases of the public good problem familiar to market theorists; that is to say, collective goods do not constitute a separate source of intrinsic value to validate government action, they are valuable because people perceive them as valuable but cannot generate them through market exchanges. If there were collective values other than those subjectively experienced by individuals then would that not give the state the moral authority to implement them for that reason alone? But this would, of course, be perfectionism and the abandonment of libertarian neutrality. The libertarian maintains that so far from there being objective collective values, as perfectionism implies, those that are claimed to be such are no more than the subjective values of whomsoever happens to be in charge of the machinery of government.

The problem for the libertarian is that of maintaining his belief in subjectivism and neutrality while at the same time recognizing that there is a case for public goods. Apart from the dogged anarcho-capitalist,[11] who insists that any wanted good or service, if wanted

[11] See D. Friedman, *The Machinery of Freedom* (New York: Arlington, 1973) and M. Rothbard, *The Ethics of Liberty* (New Jersey: Humanities Press, 1982). It should be pointed out that Rothbard is not a subjectivist in ethics; he believes that an objective natural law is the ultimate foundation of anarcho-capitalism, see *Ethics of Liberty*, 1–26.

intensely enough, will be provided by the exchange system, all libertarians recognize the necessity for a public realm: but how can that be consistent with subjectivism when the only mechanism for registering tastes, the market, has been removed?

There are certain sorts of goods which have characteristics which make them incapable of being supplied by the market.[12] The two characteristics are: *non-rivalness* in consumption (the consumption by one person does not reduce the supply available to others: compare, for example, the consumption of a bar of chocolate with that of the information supplied by a light-house) and *non-excludability* or the free-ridden problem (once supplied the good or service cannot be denied to those who do not pay for it). It is this latter feature which is of crucial importance to libertarian subjectivism since its presence encourages individuals to conceal their true preferences. The problem of the supply of a public good is a paradigm case of the Prisoner's Dilemma: a phenomenon in which rational, self-interested action leads to outcomes not desired by the very same rational self-interested individuals. Everybody, it is assumed would like clean air, but each profit-maximizing factory-owner cannot rely on the others to keep a bargain to refrain from polluting the atmosphere; furthermore, large numbers of people cannot combine effectively to sue the factory owners.[13] Indeed, the legal system itself is a public good. Again, most people, including libertarians, would feel better if avoidable distress were alleviated, but the difference one person's voluntary contribution to welfare makes is so infinitesimally small that he has no incentive to make it. With a little ingenuity it is possible to extend the range of public goods almost indefinitely. Is not the liberal order itself a public good?

Most neoclassical welfare economists justify the activity of the state on the grounds of market failure but it is difficult to sustain this and retain a belief in libertarian subjectivism. For if state activity is legitimate because it expresses people's preferences, how can it be known what those preferences are?[14] What is proposed in the state solution to the public good problem is a curious kind of 'voluntary coercion' which on the face of it is no more acceptable to the libertarian than the coercion implicit in that perfectionist political programme he is so

[12] For an introduction to public good theory, see y. Ng, *Welfare Economics* (London: Macmillan, 1979).

[13] However, see R. H. Coase, 'The Problem of Social Cost', *Journal of Law and Economics*, **3** (1960), 1–44, for a theory of how conventional 'externalities' may be 'internalised' within the rules of a common law system.

[14] It is this point which gives 'anarcho-capitalism' some intellectual plausibility, however remote the doctrine might be from political reality; see N. P. Barry, *On Classical Liberalism and Libertarianism* (London: Macmillan, 1986), Ch. 9.

anxious to condemn in others. Does some libertarian legislator have knowledge of people's preferences for public goods? Clearly not. Indeed, it is the 'knowledge problem' which for economic liberals provides a sound justification for the market in the first place.

To retain his subjectivism and neutrality the libertarian, in the presence of market failure, has to rely on some procedure analogous to the market for expresing preferences. A voting procedure is the obvious candidate for the supply of public goods: it is a choice mechanism the outcomes of which are unpredictable and in principle it rests on the assumption that no one person or group of persons has a prior knowledge of what is good for a community. However, the libertarian critique of contemporary western democracies has centred on the fact that simple majority rule procedures have tended to be inefficient transmission mechanisms for the production of genuine public goods.[15] Thus one important critical strand of libertarianism is a theory of institutions; an explanation of the way in which under some political rules an order of individuals held together by abstract rules becomes an organization directed towards a specific purpose.

Libertarian positive social science compares choice in the economic market with choice in the political market.[16] For leaving aside the important question of inequality of access to resources, about which there is understandable dispute, there is a firm consensus amongst libertarians that a market does have considerable co-ordinating properties. I say 'co-ordinating' rather than maximizing some fictitious aggregate welfare function, since the former highlights the opportunity for individual autonomy that an exchange system offers: its value is individualistic rather than collective. However, because of the nature of competition in the political market the co-ordination that does take place there is consistent with outcomes which individuals themselves may come to regret, as in the case of orthodox public good theory. In a system of legislative sovereignty, with few institutional constraints on what a government is permitted to do, competition for office by political parties produce policies that satisfy the interests of individuals as members of private groups rather than as members of an anonymous public. It is this process, it is said, which has led governments in western democracies to produce *private* goods rather than genuine *public* goods (it is the latter which is the rationale for government in all libertarian political theory). That the process can sometimes be reversed is actually a feature of that instability and inherent volatility of

[15] See, S. Brittan, 'The Economic Contradictions of Democracy', *British Journal of Political Science*, **5** (1971), 129–60.

[16] J. Schumpeter was the first to make this comparison; see his *Capitalism, Socialism and Democracy*, 5th ed. (London: Allen & Unwin, 1976).

democratic political orders; at least in comparison to market orders. Thus it is that a libertarian order of individuals co-ordinated by abstract rules is almost imperceptibly driven towards an organization: government ceases to be an enforcer of the rules but an active participant in the market. Yet the mechanism that brings this about is the very same individualistic self-interest of libertarian theory. What the libertarian wants is a different set of institutional arrangements, one more restrictive of public choice than simple majority-rule democracy, but how can he achieve this given his assumptions? Surely, a set of political rules is itself a public good?

There is then an unresolved tension between libertarianism and politics. Before I consider the suggested ways in which this might be resolved, it is important to consider briefly the contemporary objection to the metaphysics of man that lies behind the libertarian model of society. The communitarian[17] or 'republican' critique is that it is the dominance of the individualistic concept of personal agency and a concomitant theory that attributes little or no intrinsic value to traditions and denies the relevance of common purposes to politics that has created a culture in which public institutions, instead of sustaining those traditions and purposes, become the prey of a ravaging self-interest. If the predominant 'ideology' holds that people's freedom and autonomy can only be realized through the anonymous exchange relationship, with political institutions relegated to the role of instrumental conveniences, then it is surely plausible to argue that they will be exploited rather than revered. If the self of libertarian theory has no public dimension, if reason is mere calculation, as the libertarian tradition implies, then that *rational morality* which is required to sustain an order is impossible to achieve. In Alasdair Macintyre's words, liberal individualists have refused to learn from Aristotle that 'one cannot think for *oneself*, that it is only by participation in rational practice-based community that one becomes rational'.[18] It is a rich and strange irony that the logic of public choice theory, with its paraphernalia of Prisoners' Dilemmas and 'public good traps', reaches a similar conclusion to the Aristotelian Macintyre, i.e. the instability of liberal individualistic democratic regimes. The difference is that the libertarian wants a new set of rules, Macintyre a new political language.

I think that the conceptual and ethical point at issue concerns the roles of coercion and autonomy. The libertarian understands every

[17] For communitarian critique of individualism, see M. Sandel, 'The Procedural Republic and the Unencumbered Self', *Political Theory*, **12** (1984), 81–96.

[18] 'The Inadequacies of Rootless Liberalism', *The Independent* (4 February 1989). For a thorough analysis, see A. Macintyre, *Whose Justice? Which Rationality?* (London: Duckworth, 1988).

interventionist act of government, other than those required to satisfy private desires for public goods, as necessarily coercive and destructive of autonomy. The communitarian, because, he understands autonomy in a wider sense than anonymous exchange, would not regard as coercive an intervention that sustains communal values precisely because individual autonomy is as much realized through public life as it is in private experiences.

A trite example might illustrate the point: the operation of untrammeled and impersonal market forces often creates unemployment in communities which have traditional ways of life and public values through which abstract persons can become autonomous and identifiable citizens. If the state plays no positive role here then those citizens become, it is claimed anomic entities, devoid of communal identity and alienated from those abstract rules which are supposed to hold them together. From the communitarian point of view, a subsidy to declining industries, although obviously redistributive, would not be coercive. In fact, the libertarian might even, in a devious way, concede the point but translate it into his own individualistic language; heavy unemployment could cause riots, which are indiscriminate in their effects and therefore public bads, indeed they may be public bads which cannot be corrected by the conventional law and order apparatus of the state.[19]

I said earlier that the libertarian idea of an abstract social order may be a cultural achievement: that the acceptance of the blind impersonal forces of the market and the submission to abstract rules is much more a product of fortunate historical circumstances than either 'reason' or individual progress. But this is not the communitarian's argument at all. He believes that so far from being a gift to be prized, the anonymous individualist's order is the fatal error of modernism which, if not eradicated, will make any genuine kind of political life impossible.

Yet the communitarian's contention here surely rests on the implausible assumption that there are objective common standards of value which can function as some unique court of appeal on political and normative questions; some intrinsically valuable goals about which we cannot be indifferent compared to the private goals pursued, and results achieved, about which, the libertarian claims, we must necessarily be indifferent. This is not to say that the libertarian does not value a tradition: indeed the apparent disintegration of *traditional* abstract and purpose-independent rules is a cause of deep regret to him, but he would argue that in a modern society it is conceivable that there can be agreement only about the abstract rules. To suppose that there are intrinsically valuable goods is an illusion, and the attempt to make that

---

[19] A further individualist implication of this is that such government action might itself increase the propensity to riot.

illusion into a reality leads to a closure of the open market and the open society.

The example of *justice* is most germane to this issue; for undoubtedly the change from an abstract, impersonal rule-based order to a directed form of society with a common purpose, which the libertarian claims to have detected in modern society, is sanctioned by an appeal to *social* justice. However, libertarians since Adam Smith have defined justice very narrowly; as the rules of fairness, impartiality and rules that confer entitlements on legitimately acquired property. They are commutative and to that extent that they facilitate exchange, e.g. the law of contract; and they sanction force solely for the correction of past wrongs. The concept, it is claimed, has no evaluative role in the assessment of patterns of distribution that occur from the following of such rules. The libertarian insists that we must be indifferent to such patterns or outcomes precisely because there can be no agreement about socially just or ideal patterns in an advanced society: although there may be in intimate, face-to-face communities. Evaluations based on deserts and needs, as opposed to value in exchange, it is claimed, can be no more than the arbitrary decisions of centralized authority.

It is noticeable that liberal writers, such as Rawls, who differ most dramatically from libertarians on just this issue, construct forms of redistribution not from an appeal to community values but from typically individualistic devices such as hypothetical social contracts. Nevertheless, the libertarian argument against social justice even when structured in this way would still turn upon the impossibility of securing agreement on end-state redistributive principles. The redistributive principle in Rawl's work seems to be chosen by anonymous agents only because the author has so designed the contractual setting that they are bound to choose it.[20]

It should be stressed in all this that the libertarian objection to social justice is not merely utilitarian, i.e. that the continued redistribution of income has misallocational effects which work to the detriment of ultimately all the members of an anonymous society, including the worst-off. It depends as much on more overtly ethical questions about the nature of justice and the possibility of acquiring the knowledge, e.g. of deserts and needs, which is necessary for the demonstration of an alternative distribution to that produced by impersonal forces. There is no consideration of the effect that glaring inequalities may have on communal values, those are defined away. All that is suggested is that competitive processes will tend to reduce inequalities.

[20] This change has often been levelled against Rawl's contractarianism, see B. Barry, *The Liberal Theory of Justice* (Oxford: Clarendon Press, 1973), Ch. 9.

However plausible those considerations may be in relation to the evaluations of the outcomes of exchange processes (or refusal to evaluate them), they are of no help in the appraisal of property rights (and the unequal distribution of resources that accompany them) that emerge from *other* than markets, or voluntary gifts. I have said earlier that, since a market must logically begin with objects that are acquired through methods other than exchange, there must be some alternative explanation of the legitimacy of these original holdings. It is a weakness, quite possibly a crippling one, in libertarian social philosophy that its attenuated morality, its subjectivism and rejection of collective goods other than technical public goods, seems to be quite incapable of providing a theory of the justice of original holdings.

This is evidenced by the quite astonishing range of individualistic theories that have been used to justify the initial distribution of resources. Nozick uses a modified and not very satisfactory version of Locke's 'labour entitlement' theory;[21] James Buchanan, the most subjectivist of all individualists (indeed he is an avowed Hobbesian), believes that, in a state of nature, force is as good a title as labour, and suggests that even in civil society there may be legitimate redistributions in accordance with changes in the distribution of power in that society;[22] Hayek, in a convoluted version of utilitarianism, argues that we have to accept the existing distribution of resources, including inheritance, since we can never know the consequences of interfering with it.[23] There is also a tradition that sees no objection to reshuffling the pack of initial resources according to egalitarian principles as long as inequality is allowed to continue from that point.[24] From a tradition of thought that trades so heavily on the prospect of agreement, the extent of the dissent on this issue amongst its leading spokesmen is alarming.

There are other questions of pressing moral concern where libertarianism seems to provide highly controversial answers. There are special cases where exchange between individuals enhancing their subjectively perceived good offends against quite plausible conceptions of collective moral good. Should there be 'free trade' between the supplier of addictive drugs and his customer merely because both are willing? What autonomy is there in this exchange, one might well ask? Though it has to be conceded that the purely utilitarian arguments for allowing

[21] Nozick, *Anarchy, State and Utopia*, 178–82.

[22] J. Buchanan, *The Limits of Liberty* (University of Chicago, 1975), Ch. 2.

[23] F. A. Hayek, *The Constitution of Liberty* (London: Routledge and Kegan Paul, 1960), 89–91.

[24] Libertarians who take this view normally concentrate on *land*: this is a non-augmentable resource which yields a rent to its lucky owners. The early Herbet Spencer believed that the existing distribution of holdings was unjust; see his *Social Statics* (London: William and Norgate, 1854).

this have a certain plausibility. Again, should people be allowed to sell vital bodily organs merely because such deals are Pareto-efficient in the libertarian economist's sense? It has even been suggested that the 'sale' of babies from families in poor circumstances to rich, childless couples, is permissible precisely because it satisfies individual desires.

It is plausible to suggest that the libertarian's individualistic and subjective morality and neutrality disables him from making any contribution to these debates. Of course an extreme natural rights theorist would no doubt say that it would be an invasion of individual sovereignty if these exchanges were prevented. The general response, however, is to maintain a distinction between enforceable moral rules, e.g. the rules of procedural justice, and those that cannot, or ought not, to be enforced. It is not that we cannot make any moral judgments in the above cases, but that such judgments must be of the supererogatory kind. It would also be argued that if there is a common collective good that would condemn exchanges of the above type, then this might be more effectively sustained by informal pressures than by coercion. Contrary to the views ascribed to them by communitarians, libertarians are not indifferent to morality or the existence of common moral standards: but it is argued that they are complex, evolving phenomena, the implications of which are not easily discernible and hence inappropriate for peremptory legislation.

IV

I should like to return to the original problem: that of the viability of political order itself and of public goods under typical subjectivist assumptions of libertarian political theory. Libertarianism is above all a critical social theory, indeed it is radically critical of many existing institutions and practices of western democracy. Its major concern has, historically, been in delineating the respective roles of the individual and the state according to 'rational' principles. The problem with the simple majority voting rule is that it is self-defeating from a libertarian point of view: political action always seems to lead to the imposition of states of affairs on individuals, even though they result from their subjective choices. Apart from those utopians who would abolish politics entirely, libertarians accept the necessity for a public realm and yet its existence seems to offend against their principles of neutrality, minimum coercion, and the idea of a purposeless yet orderly society. Are not the communitarians and republicans right in their argument that societies are held together by common purposes, in their claim that the minimum coercion principle is far too strict for the appraisal of political life, and in their point that personal autonomy depends as much on the existence of collective goods as on individual exchange?

the minimum coercion principle is far too strict for the appraisal of political life, and in their point that personal autonomy depends as much on the existence of collective goods as on individual exchange?

There have been (at least) three notable attempts by libertarian thinkers to solve these conceptual problems: they are natural rights theories, contractarian constitutionalism, and the rather ambitious extension of the anti-rationalist spontaneous order theory of the market to the political sphere. I shall try to show that none of them is satisfactory.

Nozick is the most dominant of the rights theorists but he is by no means the only one. Most take the Kantian deontological view that forbids any state action which uses one person's life, liberty or property on behalf of another, irrespective of any consequentialist considerations. It is not strictly subjectivist since rights are assumed to be superior to any ethics that might entail their violation (however minor): it simply enjoins the state to be strictly neutral between the interest of individuals who are the bearers of equal rights. These rights do not arise from agreements, conventions and social relations between individuals but are simply those forbearances which we are universally entitled to expect from others.

However, no one has satisfactorily demonstrated the compelling nature of such abstract rights; indeed it is meaningless to speak of rights outside the context of specific social phenonema, such as promises. If having a right is exclusive sovereignty over ones own person, as opposed to being the beneficiary of some particular agreement, then some very illiberal outcomes, such as voluntary slave contracts, would be consistent with it. Furthermore, it is difficult, as A. K. Sen has shown by intriguing examples,[25] to make plausible the doctrine of the inviolability of rights, since sometimes this can result in catastrophic outcomes. Indeed, Nozick himself uses a utilitarian argument to justify private and exclusive land ownership (which might be excluded by his modified Lockean entitlement theory) when he argues that that form of ownership ensures higher productivity from which everybody benefits.[26]

More generally, the attempt to fix for all time the contents of a list of 'rights' is not quite consistent with the libertarian idea of the unknowability of the future: thus we cannot know in advance what rights are appropriate for an individualist society. These are as much a matter of discovery, through the exercise of, to use Adam Smith's

[25] A. K. Sen, 'The Moral Standing of the Market', in *Ethnics and Economics*, Ellen Frankel Paul, Fred Miller and Jeffrey Paul (eds), (Oxford: Blackwell, 1985), 1–19.

[26] Nozick, *Anarchy, State and Utopia*, 177.

codes creates the misleading impression that the list of rights is exhausted by the contents of the code.

Irrespective of all this, rights theorists (with the exotic exception of anarcho-capitalists) do justify a state. But surely its very existence, i.e. a body with a monopoly of coercive power, implies an inequality of rights no matter how limited it might be? Nozick tries to show that his state does not violate rights, but not to anyone's satisfaction.[27]

Contractarian constitutionalism is perhaps the most intriguing libertarian doctrine, since it is the most subjectivist of all, especially as found in the political philosophy of James Buchanan.[28] Here we find neutrality pushed to its limits; for it is argued that moral values have no cognitive status, they are the subjective preferences of individuals: moral and political 'truth' is a matter of *agreement*, not a product of reason or an 'objective' natural law or natural rights (*pace* Nozick). Thus liberalism, libertarianism, or any other 'ism' has no claim to validity unless it is agreed to by individuals. There are no collective moral goods through which people may express their individual autonomy, though there are public goods for which people express a preference through a formal procedure. Any attempt to implement things politically because they are of intrinsic value would simply be an attempt to impose one set of subjective preferences on others.

In fact, what Buchanan is really getting at is the attempt made by his fellow liberal welfare economists to find objective solutions to public good problems, e.g. by 'arbitrarily' imposing a tax to close the gap between marginal private and marginal social cost in the presence of some externality. However, the alleged welfare losses due to externalities must be an entirely subjective matter and hence not amenable to precise calculation. Again, there is no such thing as an 'optimal' supply of public goods, for decisions about this must be equally subjective. The only way in which subjective choice can be expressed are either through markets or voting and if their rules are generally acceptable the outcomes must be acceptable, i.e. the state remains neutral. In the subjectivist view, the democratic state is not neutral because its simple majority voting rule only allows a narrow range of choices to be expressed.

Buchanan is a contractarian because he argues that anonymous individuals in an hypothetical state of nature would agree to more restrictive rules than those that obtain at present, in order to prevent their

---

[27] See Barry, *On Classical Liberalism and Libertarianism*, Ch. 8.

[28] For Buchanan's political philosophy, see *The Limits of Liberty*, and also his *Freedom in Constitutional Contract* (Austin: A & M University Press, 1977). For a critique, see N. P. Barry, 'Agreement, Unanimity and Liberalism', *Political Theory*, **12** (1984), 579–96.

interests being over-ridden. Buchanan's libertarianism is entirely procedural and the state remains neutral only when it is bound by strict rules, which are themselves the product of subjective choice. It could supply public goods under a procedure of less than unanimity (e.g. a two-thirds majority rule for efficiency reasons) but this would be legitimate only if it were agreed to at the contractual stage.[29]

In fact, Buchanan commits a startling piece of intellectual suicide, for by excluding all intrinsic goods, including liberal ones such as free markets and the rule of law, unless they are agreed to by individuals, he makes the transition to the free society he favours virtually impossible. If all values are subjective, then the choices of individuals for a non-liberal order have equal weight with those that favour one: to move from a *status quo* which is non-liberal to a liberal one without general consent would be a case of perfectionism and therefore condemnable. Buchanan's social philosophy represents perhaps the *reductio ad absurdum* of anti-perfectionist libertarian individualism. Since nothing is intrinsically right, any change from the *status quo* could be vetoed by any one person (unless he could be bought out). This subjectivist libertarianism ends up as a rigid conservatism, albeit from the most unconservative of premises.

It is because of the libertarian's acceptance of the necessity for some public action and his refusal to accept anything as intrinsically right that the libertarian is driven to those elaborate contractarian constructions in order to make government action consistent with subjective choice. Under the subjectivist criteria one wonders how any rules ever become legitimate?

Yet clearly they do. A whole range of institutions, including the common law and those constitutional and other rules for the servicing of a market system, have evolved and become accepted over time and yet a contract never validated them. They do not contain universal 'rights'; and though a process of evolution has generated rights to property and exchange and so on these derive from social relationships and would appear to have little to do with an active reason. Though such public rules are not all 'neutral' in the strict sense implied by rationalistic libertarians, they have been sufficiently abstract to accommodate an enormous variety of individual ends and purposes in open societies. Yet how could they have emerged and been sustained, given

---

[29] Buchanan argues that rational individuals would be more likely to chose the two thirds majority rule than simple majority rule because, although it would harm their interests on some occasions, over a run of political decisions, its application would produce collective benefits; see his Nobel Prize Lecture, 'The Constitution of Economic Policy', *American Economic Review*, LXXVII (1987), 243–50.

societies. Yet how could they have emerged and been sustained, given the typical individualist assumptions and given the apparent omnipresence of Prisoners' Dilemmas? Why has not subjectivism always produced the Hobbesian state?

It may well be the case that Prisoners' Dilemmas are solved, without the invocation of a Hobbesian sovereign, all the time without people being consciously aware of it. It is well-known theoretically that in repeated plays of the Prisoners' Dilemma game, agreements which are to the mutual benefit of the parties will be kept if individuals employ a tit-for-tat strategy, i.e. each will retaliate if the other breaks an agreement. If people are prepared to initiate co-operative activity then the advantages of promise-keeping, respect for property rights and so on, will become readily apparent.[30] Defection from agreements becomes a mug's game.

It is not at all implausible to suppose that the law of contract emerged in this way without being consciously planned. Indeed, many small communities, of a socialist and anarchist kind, have historically provided welfare and public services to their members by a similar rationale. None of these 'collective goods' have anything to do with 'intrinsic values'. Indeed, the explanation of the emergence of these practices has much more in common with Hume's account of moral *conventions* than with Aristotelian communitarianism.

Enticing though this explanation is for some libertarians, it has obvious disadvantages. For one thing, mutual co-operation between self-interested agents for the production of public goods is likely only when the supply of that good depends on their co-operation; the disbenefits of defection from agreements are obvious to all. However, in modern societies, a public good, once supplied, is available to all whether they have contributed or not. Hence, mass defection is the more likely consequence so that in the absence of coercion the good will not be supplied at all. 'Large numbers' are as much of a problem for libertarians as they were for Rousseau.

Another serious problem is that evolutionary processes do not always produce rules and practices that are amenable to the libertarian. There are many rules which nobody designed that are not individualistic. This is why rationalistic natural rights doctrines have such an appeal to libertarians, despite the implausibility of their foundations.

The conclusion must be that libertarian assumptions, encompassing subjectivism, neutrality, anti-perfectionism and so on, ultimately fail to explain the kind of social order libertarians favour. Perhaps, property, the rule of law, and free markets are, after all, intrinsically valuable. But I do not know how that could be demonstrated to someone who thought otherwise.

[30] For an intriguing development of these ideas, see R. Sugden, *The Economics of Rights, Co-operation and Welfare* (Oxford: Blackwell, 1986).

Conclusion

A. PHILLIPS-GRIFFITHS

A rough and tumble, we have had; though one quite lacking in impoliteness. I hope I do not go too far in supplying that deficiency.

Political Syllogisms

Disagreement is endemic on political questions, both between and within ourselves. We do however come to conclusions, often strongly held. It may often be in doing so we are wholly irrational; but in so far as we are not, the philosopher should surely have something to contribute?

Our conclusions, so far as they are at all rational conclusions, will be based on some considerations or other: our *premises*. So, it may be thought, so far as we are rational we should be clear about what our premises are, how if at all they may be justified, and that our conclusions logically follow from them. Only if this is so are our conclusions justified.

Enoch Powell uses the language appropriate to this way of looking at it; he says what

> underlies most political discourse—the assumption of addressing those who are peers not only in the sense that, of course, by their vote collectively they hold the power to give you what you want or to withhold it, but peers in the sense that they can be addressed upon the basis of common unstated assumptions. That is the major premise from which, by the application of explicit minor premises, all conclusions are drawn in political discourse.

This assumption, he says, forms the major premise of a syllogism. But I am not sure he means only that: he also seems to be suggesting that it is the 'common unstated assumptions' which function as the major premise of a syllogism from which political conclusions are drawn by applying minor premises.

What is a syllogism? I claim that one day my dog, Fido, will die. Challenged by a sceptic, I argue impeccably as follows:

(1) All dogs will die
(2) Fido is a dog
(3) Therefore Fido will die (Q.E.D.)

Premise (1) is just the sort of thing which might be regarded as a common unstated assumption (people do not waste time telling each other that, unless it is to very small children); and what I do is remind my doubter of it, relying on my identity of introspection with him.

This is a typical syllogism. The word 'syllogism' is derived, not from the Old English sælig (happy) but from one or other of the Greek verbs συλλογιξεσθαι (to reckon) and συλλογτη (to collect). The latter is perhaps more illuminating, as we can think of the major premise (1) as *collecting* together a whole lot of things (dogs) under a general heading 'what will die', and then in, the minor premise (2) stating that Fido is one of those things, and hence falls under the general heading.

The relation between premises and conclusion is strictly logical, and can be formalized: as Aristotle, and in a much fuller way, medieval logicians, set out to do.

What, it may be asked, has all this to do with politics? The answer is, nothing much.

Robert Skidelsky and Kenneth Minogue, nevertheless, share the view that political discourse does depend on some common, often unconscious assumptions. Minogue regards it as the business to examine and explore these assumptions, to avoid muddle; and of that, more later. Neither, however, regard them as 'major premises' from which political conclusions can be logically deduced. As Skidelsky most tellingly puts it: '. . . politics does not take place at this level of introspection; that which makes politics possible is not what politics is about'. What makes it possible for me to put the argument about my dog to you, are the publishing facilities of the Cambridge University Press. But that is not what the argument is about.

It may, of course, be at least true that some particular arguments are incompatible with those assumptions, and this may need making clear. But again, more of that later.

However, it might be thought, even if these assumptions are not the 'major premises' on which political arguments must rest, there must be some: and, of course, if they do not rest on this (unquestioned, and, if constitutive, unquestionable bedrock) the problem arises of how they are to be justified. It may be that even more specific questions than those relating to the very possibility of political discourse still have to be represented in this way.

Again Powell uses the language which would be appropriate if this were so.

I was feeling my way towards understanding the axiom of government subject to parliamentary representation, namely that such government cannot logically extend over a population which cannot be there represented. It was the old proposition of the American

Colonies, (by which I was later to understand that my own country had been haunted for the best part of two centuries).

An *axiom* about what is *logically* impossible? Was there one? For two centuries? My grandmother was one of the first women to get the vote, when she was about 48 years old. Did a situation obtain for 200 years which was nevertheless logically impossible? No: 'being represented' does not mean 'having a vote'. Women were *virtually* represented (some more so than others, like politician's mistresses in France). As were children; and, possibly, even dogs. But, it seems, not Bengalis. (But had they no one to speak for them? Undoubtedly, had he not been too late, Mr Powell would have done.) The old proposition of the American Colonies was 'No taxation without representation'. Did that allow that there need be no representation without taxation? Parliamentary representation was, after all, denied far less than 200 years ago to those without 'a (property) stake in the country', unless we say the others enjoyed virtual representation. Indeed, much later than that, local government representation was denied to businesses despite their being heavily taxed, for the sake of democracy. If a population is to be represented, *who* in the population is to be represented? And how? By having a vote, or by being the servant of someone who has a vote? And are the Scottish and Welsh minorities properly represented at Westminster? Neither has the kind of equal group representation, as against the English, which is being advocated by some for the white minority in South Africa, as against the blacks.

These matters do not seem open and closed; but if we are going to speak of axioms here, we had better have some definitions: and 'representation' does not seem to have the right sort of definition, and, if Kant is right, it could not have (at least that is what he said of the concept of 'right' in jurisprudence). The issues are serious: but some clever dick might make a mockery of them if we treat them as theorems in an axiomatic system.

This seems to go deeper in Powell's account than a mere choice of terms. He says:

> upon the whole, things are wiser than people, . . . institutions are wiser than their members and that a nation is wiser than those who comprise it at any specific moment.

This seems to be the major premise, from which

> To my own satisfaction, I reached the conclusion that the price mechanism is one of the means by which a society takes certain collective decisions in a manner not necessarily ideal, but a manner which is acceptable and broadly speaking regarded as workable, a mechanism which cannot safely or wisely be replaced by conscious formulation or compulsion.

with the consequence that

> I found myself engaged in a fundamental critique of the whole theory
> of trade unions, since this was the use of coercion in order to produce
> a different price for an article from that which would be placed on it
> by supply and demand.

This view was taken over by the Conservative Party in the late sixties,
and has now taken over Hungary, Czechoslovakia and possibly even
Brandenburg, if not Brussels. How is it that it is shared by so many who
would find such a major premise unacceptable? (Are such institutions
as Trade Unions and the British Medical Association wiser than their
members? If the nation is wiser than those who comprise it at any
moment, at which moment was the British nation wiser: when they
approved of cossetting Trade Union leaders with beer and sandwiches,
or when they give them the disapproving cold shoulder?)

How could such a very disparate set of people as Powell, Hayek,
Minogue, Benn (Sir Ernest), Pinochet, and Mrs Thatcher have all
shared this 'commonality' based on such a premise? And, for that
matter, I, who do not (consciously) accept this premise? Having been
much taken with Spencer's *The Man Versus the State* at school, I was
further encouraged on reading Hayek's *The Road to Serfdom* in 1948.
Through all those awful sixties, the commonality I came across made
me feel that my voice, when I raised it at all, was like one crying in the
wilderness; whereas now, in line with my juvenile prejudices of 1945, a
deep admirer of Mrs Thatcher as the greatest and most liberal Prime
Minister since Gladstone, I sound like a conventional old bore. It
rather bothers me: I was happier when I was in a small minority. Must I
think that what was at work in each of us was the Zeitgeist (one pretty
temporary, as Don Locke suggests), disguising itself in whatever intellectual clothes we each found acceptable?

Fundamental Assumptions

Where, then, are we to get our fundamental premises for political
argument, and what form can they take? The shared, not always
common assumptions, to which Powell, Minogue and Skidelsky all
refer cannot serve this purpose. However, it is suggested that they
influence our thought, and that it may be muddles about them which
lead us to conclusions incompatible with them or not demanded by
them. So, says Minogue, it is the business of the philosopher to bring
them to light and clarify them. There is, however, a profound difficulty
here. It is one raised by some of Wittgenstein's views in his *On Certainty* and elsewhere. We can dispute and disagree within a language

game, within a range of accepted concepts; and there is no common language game, no accepted concept, unless there is some agreement in judgments. But in the philosophical literature, disagreement about supposed principles of this sort are as nothing compared with whether they *are*, or indeed whether there need be *any*, principles of this sort.[1]

Commissioner Lin, administering South China in the 1830s and 40s, found it impossible to convince the British merchants, and Queen Victoria,[2] that they should stop flooding his country with opium: *nothing he could say had any effect*. So he decided on force: but his resources were small, so he sent some social anthropologists to England to find out what our weaknesses were in order that he could attack them. They found, to their surprise, that not all the English were impervious to argument; a few even in Government were not; but, they reported, these had not been able to get enough tickets. They were able to find the weakness, and advocated that all supplies of dried rhubarb should be cut off, which would debilitate us all by constipation. But they were also mightily puzzled by the fact that nobody in England exposed their infant daughters on mountainsides; and concluded that this must be because the English were very short of people. Is there nothing that could ever be said to the Chinese against infanticide, as Lin thought nothing could be said to the English about destroying people through the opium trade? Might not there have been a few Chinese without (for the time being) enough tickets?

I am of course far from suggesting that the solution to political predicaments can be found in rational argument. The question here is not whether there may be points at which it *does* break down, but whether there is a point where for purely conceptual reasons it *must* break down. Thus Skidelsky quotes Powell:

> Politics in the last resort is about the life and death of nations, about what nations are, about how they change, how they grow, how they perish or are destroyed. It is for this that the individuals who compose nations lived and died; it is with this that their strongest and deepest emotions and passions are intertwined.

This may be true, as a matter of psychological fact, in certain times and places; it looks frighteningly plausible in Azerbaijan and Georgia and Lithuania now that the *Pax Russiana* has failed. However, I do have

---

[1] Renford Bambrough discusses this and related issues in his 'Fools and Heretics', in *Wittgenstein: Centenary Essays*, Royal Institute of Philosophy Supplements (Cambridge University Press, forthcoming).

[2] Lin's letter to Queen Victoria asked her to consider how she would regard traders who were selling her subjects dangerous drugs: which is hardly an exotic moral appeal. There is no record of any reply.

reason to hope that my Welsh cousin Mr Neil Kinnock is right in thinking that he has introspected our Welsh commonality concerning this matter as effectively as Tonypandy did. But perhaps, if it were not that commonality, it would be another. But who knows what it is? If there is one, Powell is right in saying that a politician who swims against it will fail and he will make progress better if he goes with its tide; but there may be other reasons for failing (as in the tragic case of Dilke) and other explanations for relative success (as at first in the case of Horatio Bottomley, though he, unlike so many others, was found out). So we cannot know when someone has the spirit of the people even after the event. Skidelsky says '. . . commonality is what makes politics possible. When it is not there, you have war'. There must be other occasions of armed conflict, as students of the origins of the Lilliputian war are aware. Could it be that, where commonality is not, there is nevertheless *no* war? Not if commonality is as essential an ingredient of peaceful political life as that *virtus dormitiva* which must be present in any substance if it is to put us to sleep.

Equality

But there may be other principles, distinct from and perhaps prior to or overriding with regard to what is contained, albeit covertly, in the commonality, which would serve us as fundamental premises; such as the Principle of Equality.

David Miller has made us very wary of that: he shows how difficult it is to formulate any principle which is both practicable and acceptable. But he may be willing nevertheless to place this in the unquestionable bedrock of political thinking. 'If there is indeed an important sense in which egalitarianism is written into contemporary conditions of life, it makes no sense to think of oneself as taking a stand for or against equality.' Minogue agrees this far: equality, at least in certain forms— equality of manners, equality before the law, and belief in an immortal soul—are the '*presuppositions* of our way of life'. David Miller, however, is more cautious in his specification of its content. 'The conflict is not about equality as such, but about competing specifications of that value, about different versions of what it means to treat people as equals.' This certainly makes it much more plausible to claim that giving value to equality is an essential part of the commonality, or at any rate much more difficult to show that it is not.

However, I am being rather unfair to Miller here: at least he says what is now taken for granted, as indeed does Minogue, which in past times was not; and what he does is to develop, most carefully and while exhibiting all the difficulties, a notion of a value, or principle of equality, or social ideal of equality, which could be both appealing and viable. It may also be that Minogue is unfair in criticizing Miller on the grounds that even his somewhat attenuated notion of equality (necessarily attenuated because of the difficulties of practicality and acceptability which Miller clearly exhibits) is something which should be *legislated*. What Miller advocates is a certain social attitude—the mutual respect which comes from according equality of status—which he certainly does not think can be legislated into existence. However, he does suggest that the development of this desirable attitude may be to some degree prevented by great inequalities of wealth (an empirical claim about which Minogue is sceptical); and that therefore the fostering of equality may require a certain direction in 'public policy'. I am not sure how fair it would be to object to this: since Miller says, at least with regard to his discussion of 'simple equality', that 'in pursuing this question I shall not be concerned with difficulties that are frequently raised about the compatibility of equality with other values such as economic efficiency and personal liberty'. Minogue's objections are in terms of personal liberty. Unfortunately, in that discussion, Miller, avoiding the surreal—'science fiction carried on by other means'—has to consider just that. He says of one egalitarian proposal:

> Either we allow people to reap the full benefits of their personal capacities and end up with a society that is quite inegalitarian in its distribution of resources (and presumably of welfare too); or we attempt to correct for inequalities of talent and end up with what has been called with some hyperbole 'the slavery of the talented'—slavery to society because of their own productive potential.

But, personal liberty being put on one side, what is wrong with slavery?

The difficulty arises perhaps because one is not sure whether what is being considered is a 'value', a 'principle', or a 'social ideal'. Minogue and Miller would not dispute too much about the first. To speak of this as a value is to say that it is an important consideration, among many others. To advocate it as a sole, or overriding principle would be insane: never mind at all other 'principles', such as liberty, charity, or stability? It will not do to say that these principles will also play their part, as minor premises, or in some systematic hierarchy of principles which form a deductive system. One can call them *prima facie* principles—or just relevant considerations or commonly accepted values—but that is not to say that from them we can form an algorithm which will determine the real case. Is equality, then important in founding a 'social ideal'? Will that be the same as the ideal liberal society, or the ideally benevolent society, or the ideally stable society? If so, can anyone say what it is? And if not, how do we choose between them without rejecting all of them because none measures up to the others?

A. Phillips-Griffiths

We might instead regard these considerations as suggestions for relevant criticisms, attending to real situations not ideal ones. I am conscious that this is a very conservative suggestion, treating the aim of politics, as Richard Hooker said in the sixteenth century as 'the righting of wrongs and the remedying of injustices', and putting up with a lot of inconsistency in the process.

Human Nature

In his response to Miller, Minogue accuses the egalitarian of misconstruing the nature of human beings. It may well be that many high level political theories are informed by such construals or misconstruals; and indeed that it would be impossible to make sense of some political systems of institutions unless they presuppose some very specific and definite views about the nature of humanity: for example, unless they are some unbelievably clever and monstrous trick, theocracies such as Iran or seventeenth century Geneva or even Puritan England. But it is important to be very careful not to jump into such high level considerations in the consideration of real political issues; they can lead one into major or minor premises as irrelevant as they are high-minded.

Does one have to espouse a concept of liberal man in order to cherish liberal values, a concept which misconstrues human nature? Certainly political philosophers, liberals and others, have adumbrated, or even systematized, concepts of human nature as the grounds of their positions. Important disagreements over fundamental claims are found among them.

Thus Aristotle: 'He who is by nature without the *polis* is either a beast or a God'; Marx 'It is not the individual consciousness which is prior to society, but society which is prior to individual consciousness'. On the other hand: Hobbes's geometrical deduction of the laws of nature from the simple asocial elements of man, and Mill's having more in common with Holbach and Helvetius than with Hegel, though as G. W. Smith shows, very different from both. The strange thing is that it is very difficult to relate these high level theories and metaphysical conceptions of human nature to practical differences in political controversy. Hobbes and Helvetius (the latter coming to conclusions which are similar to those attributed by Minogue to the illiberal egalitarians) could hardly be called liberals; and while trying to decide whether Aristotle was a liberal is as silly as arguing about whether Plato was a fascist, it would not be inapposite to point to the many liberal elements in Hegel and even more appositely to those of the now rarely read T. H. Green.

As for myself, I am firmly of the Aristotle–Marx (and I might add Wittgenstein) persuasion, yet nobody could be a deeper-dyed liberal. However, that is not evidence: it may simply be that I am not sufficiently philosophically competent, and that if only I could have understood Heidegger better I would have ended up a Nazi. Rather in that spirit of unfairness, I shall draw some lessons from Susan Mendus's criticisms of the liberal John Moore.

A particular passage from a speech of political persuasion by Mr John Moore is to be found on page 46 of Mendus's essay; and it was given to defend Government changes in the National Health Service. The question is how this defence is supposed to connect with what liberals 'characteristically assume', not only that we *can* control our own lives (that we are to some degree invulnerable), but that we will flourish better if we *do* control our lives (that we are, to some degree, not in need of things external to us).

I do not see how anyone could be forced to Mr Moore's advocacy of the relatively minor changes in the Government Health Service by such totally vacuous, innocuous and self-evidently true propositions, or to oppose it because of the equally innocuous truths that we cannot always control our own lives (that we are to some very considerable degree vulnerable) and that we are not always better of controlling our lives (that we are, to some degree, in need of things external to us). However, it is not the minor changes but the *spirit* of Mr Moore's remarks which Mendus takes to depend on a misconstrual of the nature of man. But the two cannot be separated. Indeed, if, as to all appearances it is the case, that Mr Moore is not insane, we would not expect him to suggest that his considerations should determine all aspects of the Health Service, and that to avoid becoming dependent we should no longer rely on others to provide us with heart transplants, but that we should do it for ourselves. One should not ignore other aspects of the context, of a particular social situation in which it is thought that people have come to expect to depend on others too much; which is surely possible, for example if I were to lie in bed all day calling to my granddaughter for cups of tea? Is it not, as Mendus suggests, a matter of degree, and not only that, of the particular circumstances? Should the considerations put forward by Mr Moore, whether or not they clinch the argument on this particular issue, never be put forward *at all*?

Mendus says that the liberal view of man is either an idealization or an abstraction. As an idealization, it is false to our lives. I would agree, with respect to all idealizations, unless there is no difference between the real and the ideal. If it is an abstraction, she says, we are not warranted in culling *this* from the process of abstraction, rather than something else. '*This*' is our capacity to choose, to act independently of others. Certainly, anyone who thought this abstraction captured everything importantly true about human beings—I have sometimes thought Sartre, though no liberal, did—could only escape the charge of being daft by being a distinguished philosopher. I have already said enough to show that I am not enamoured of such idealizations and abstractions. What should we have instead to inform (if not to form the basic premise of) our political thinking?

Perhaps not an idealization or an abstraction, but a model. Mendus offers the model of a vine, but I do not find that helpful, since it does not seem to me to capture what she wants. Man needs, like the vine, sunshine and water, if not the green dew and not always the liquid sky (being able to use artesian wells, e.g. in California); and these are things over which he has little or no control, though rather more than the vine, having umbrellas and aqueducts. But the model of the vine breaks down, which it would not if it were a toadstool or a convolvulus, because the one thing a vine imperatively needs is a gardener, preferably armed with some technology—a spade if not a tractor; and he had better be a pretty self-directed, self-controlled, responsible gardener, having some independent initiative, and more capable of looking after himself than is the vine. But some reflections on this have been put much better and more seriously by Peter Binns. The other example is from Steinbeck's fiction, and I hope Susan Mendus will not mind my using it to make a similar point about what would be, not hers, but an exaggerated criticism of Government policy.

Lennie, a homicidal imbecile, is doomed; not, however, because he is a homicidal imbecile, but because he is human. 'His fate is (potentially) the fate of us all in so far as we are vulnerable to things outside our control'. Lennie can hardly be an idealization: but neither ought he to be treated as an abstraction, for we could not be warranted in culling *this* from the process of abstraction. He must be neither, but just the way we are. I strongly believe that there is another way in which our government has failed to recognize need and dependency: in expelling near-imbeciles from asylums, to be cared for 'in the community', i.e. not at all. But this applies to all of us, for we are essentially like Lennie. Government should provide not fewer, but vastly more, lunatic asylums, for everybody.

Moral Considerations

One kind of consideration which it would seem could never be regarded as irrelevant to political discussion is moral consideration. I suppose that an amoral person, if not an immoral person, could regard them as such; but nobody with moral attitudes could, because of the nature of moral attitudes: they are not the sort of attitudes which can be abandoned. But that does not mean that moral principles could be used as major premises from which political answers could be deduced, or even that strongly held moral aims must entail the adoption of what would be effective political means. Moral considerations of a pervasive kind will surely be relevant, but the question will always be how they are relevant and in what situations. I admit I find this issue a little difficult, since I cannot easily distinguish pervasive political values—liberty and tolerance, welfare and benevolence, equality and fairness—from moral ones. Perhaps this position is more common among liberals than others; but it obviates the need to repeat what I have claimed for political considerations, with regard to moral ones. But to what degree any particular institution or practice has implications with regard to moral considerations is a question which must be approached with sceptical care: as is shown by Don Locke with regard to the institution, or practice, of the market.

Envoi

I was originally asked to comment on Norman Barry's paper, but for reasons which almost amount to excuses I failed to do so effectively at the time. I do not do so now: except that it seems to me to be an admirably closely argued case about the failure of the application of high-level, *a priori* abstractions. Like Barry, I do not know how anybody could *demonstrate* anything in this area at all.

I have contributed nothing towards the question with which I began, or to the questions of these collected papers: my comments have been uniformly negative and sceptical. Had I known at the time that I would be preparing these concluding remarks, I should have taken copious notes of the discussions of these papers, which were far better than anything I have supplied (though at least as sceptical). But it is some little while ago, and I do not remember enough; except that I went out by the same door as in I came.

Index

Index

References

Ackerman, B. A. *Social Justice in the Liberal State*. Yale University Press, 1980

Acton, H. B. *The Morals of Markets: an Ethical Exploration*. London: Longman, 1971

Arblaster, A. *The Rise and Decline of Western Liberalism*. Oxford: Blackwell, 1984

Aristotle. *Politics*. Penguin: Harmondsworth, 1962

Arneson, R. 'Equality and Equal Opportunity for Welfare', *Philosophical Studies* 54 (1988), 79–95

Bamborough, R. 'Fools and Heretics', in *Wittgenstein: Centenary Essays*, Royal Institute of Philosophy Supplement. Cambridge University Press, forthcoming

Barry, B. *The Liberal Theory of Justice*. Oxford: Clarendon Press, 1973

Barry, N. P. 'Agreement, Unanimity and Liberalism', *Political Theory*, 12 (1984)

Barry, N. P. *On Classical Liberalism and Libertarianism*. London: Macmillan, 1986

Barry, N. P. *The Invisible Hand in Economics and Politics*. London: Institute of Economic Affairs, 1988

Berger, F. R. *Happiness, Justice and Freedom: the Moral and Political Philosophy of J. S. Mill*. Berkeley: University of California Press, 1984

Berlin, I. 'Equality', *Proceedings of the Aristotelian Society* LVI (1955/6)

Berlin, I. *Four Essays on Liberty*. Oxford University Press, 1969

Bloch, M. *Feudal Society*. London: Routledge and Kegan Paul, 1965, Vol. I

Brittan, S. 'The Economic Contradictions of Democracy', *British Journal of Political Science* 5 (1971)

Buchanan, J. *Freedom in Constitutional Contract*. Austin: A & M University Press, 1977

Buchanan, J. *The Limits of Liberty*. University of Chicago, 1975

Buchanan, J. 'The Constitution of Economic Policy', *American Economic Review* LXXVII (1987)

Cirillo, R. *The Economics of Vilfredo Pareto*. London, 1979

Coase, R. H. 'The Problem of Social Cost' *Journal of Law and Economics* 3 (1960)

Cohen, G. A. 'On the Currency of Egalitarian Justice', *Ethics* 99 (1988–9), 906

Cohen, G. A. 'Self-Ownership, World-Ownership and Equality: Part II', *Social Philosophy and Policy* 3 (1985–6), 77–96

Crosland, A. *Socialism Now* London: Cape, 1974

Dent, N. 'The "tensions" of Liberalism', *Philosophical Quarterly* (October 1988)

Dworkin, R. 'Equality of Welfare', *Philosophy and Public Affairs* 10 (1981), 185–246

References

Dworkin, R. 'Equality of Resources', *Philosophy and Public Affairs* **10** (1981), 289

Flew, A. *The Politics of Procrustes*. London: Temple Smith, 1981

Friedman, D. *The Machinery of Freedom*. New York: Arlington, 1973

Gellner, E. 'The Social Roots of Egalitarianism', in *Culture, Identity and Politics*. Cambridge University Press, 1987

Gray, J. N. 'Mill's and Other Liberalisms', in K. Haakonssen (ed.), *Traditions of Liberalism: Essays on Locke, Smith and J. S. Mill*. St Leonards, NSW: Centre for Independent Studies, 1988

Gray, J. *Hayek On Liberty*, 2nd ed. Oxford: Blackwell, 1984

Griffin, J. *Well Being*. Oxford: Clarendon Press, 1986

Hayek, F. A. *The Constitution of Liberty*. London: Routledge and Kegan Paul, 1960

Hayek, F. A. *Law, Legislation and Liberty*, Vol. 2: *The Mirage of Social Justice*. London: Routledge & Kegan Paul, 1982

Hayek, F. A. *The Fatal Conceit*. London: Routledge, 1988

Hibbert, C. *The French Revolution*. Harmondsworth: Penguin, 1980

Hollis, M. *The Cunning of Reason*. Cambridge University Press, 1987

Kirzner, I. *Competition and Entrepreneurship*. University of Chicago Press, 1973

Lydall, H. *The Structure of Earnings*. Oxford: Clarendon Press, 1968

Macaulay, T. B. 'Mill's Essay on Government: Utilitarian. Logic and Politics', in J. Lively and J. Rees (eds.), *Utilitarian Logic and Politics*. Oxford: Clarendon Press, 1978

MacIntyre, A. *After Virtue*. London: Duckworth, 1981

MacIntyre, A. *Whose Justice? Which Rationality?* London: Duckworth, 1988

Malinowski, S. *Sex and Repression in Savage Society*. London: Kegan Paul, 1927

Marx, K. and Engels, F. *The German Ideology*, ed. C. Arthur. New York: International Publishers, 1970

Marx, K. *Grundrisse*. Harmondsworth: Penguin, 1973

Mill, J. S. *Principles of Political Economy, Collected Works* ed. J. M. Robson, Vol. 3. Toronto University Press, 1965

Mill, J. S. *System of Logic, Collected Works* ed. J. M. Robson, Vol. 8, Book 6. Toronto: Toronto University Press, 1969

Mill, J. S. 'Considerations on Representative Government', in H. B. Acton (ed.) *Utilitarianism; On Liberty; Representative Government*. London: Dent, 1972

Mill, J. S. *On Liberty*. Harmondsworth: Penguin, 1978

Miller, D. *Social Justice*. Oxford: Clarendon Press, 1976

Miller, D. 'Democracy and Social Justice', *British Journal of Political Science* (1978), reprinted in P. Birnbaum, J. Lively and G. Parry (eds.), *Democracy, Concensus and Social Contract*. London: Sage, 1978

Miller, D. 'Arguments for Equality', *Midwest Studies in Philosophy* Vol. VII Minneapolis: University of Minnesota Press, 1982

Miller, D. *Market, State and Community*. Oxford: Clarendon Press, 1989

Miller D. and Siedentop, L. A. *The Nature of Political Theory*. Oxford: Clarendon Press, 1983

References

Minogue, K. *The Egalitarian Conceit.* London: Centre for Policy Studies, 1989

Moore, J. Conservative Political Centre publication, October 1987

Ng, Y. *Welfare Economics.* London: Macmillan, 1979.

Nieli, R. 'Spheres of Intimacy and the Adam Smith Problem', *Journal of the History of Ideas* XLVII (1986)

Nozick, R. Anarchy, State and Utopia. Oxford: Blackwell, 1974

Nussbaum, M. *The Fragility of Goodness.* Cambridge University Press, 1986

O'Neill, O. 'Contructivisms in Ethics', *Proceedings of the Aristotelian Society* LXXXIX (1989/9)

Oakeshott, M. 'The Character of a Modern European State', in *On Human Conduct,* Oxford University Press, 1975

Pascal, B. *Pensées.* Harmondsworth: Penguin, 1976

Pashukanis, E. V. *Law and Marxism: a General Theory* ed. C. Arthur London: Ink Links, 1978

Phillips, D. Z. 'Some Limits to Moral Endeavour, in *Through a Darkening Glass.* Oxford: Blackwell, 1982

Rawls, J. *A Theory of Justice.* Oxford: Clarendon Press, 1972

Raz, J. *The Morality of Freedom.* Oxford: Clarendon Press, 1986

Roemer, J. 'Equality of Talent', *Economics and Philosophy* 1 (1985), 165

Rothbard, M. *The Ethics of Liberty.* New Jersey: Humanities Press, 1982

Sandel, M. 'The Procedural Republic and the Unencumbered Self', *Political Theory* 12 (1984), 81–96

Schumpeter, J. *Capitalism, Socialism and Democracy,* 5th ed. London: Allen & Unwin, 1976

Sen, A. K. 'The Moral Standing of the Market', in Ellen Frankel Paul, Fred Miller and Jeffrey Paul (eds.) *Ethnics and Economics.* Oxford: Blackwell, 1985

Sen, A. K. *On Ethics and Economics.* Oxford: Blackwell, 1987

Siedentop, L. A., 'Political Theory and Ideology: the case of the state, in D. Miller and L. A. Siedentop (eds.), *op cit.*

Simons H. C. *Economic Policy for a Free Society.* University of Chicago Press, 1948

Smith, A. *Lectures on Jurisprudence,* ed. R. L. Meek *et al.* Indianapolis: Liberty Press, 1982

Smith, G. W. 'The Logic of J. S. Mill on Liberty', *Political Studies* XXVIII (1980)

Spencer, H. *Social Statics.* London: William and Norgate, 1854

Steinbeck, J. *Of Mice and Men.* Reading: Pan, 1974

Steinbeck, J. *The Grapes of Wrath.* Suffolk, Pan, 1975

Sugden, R. *The Economics of Rights, Co-operation and Welfare.* Oxford: Blackwell, 1986

Tocqueville, A. de. *Democracy in America.* New York: Vintage Books, 1945, Vol. I

Waldron J. (ed.) *Nonsense Upon Stilts: Bentham, Burke and Marx on the Rights of Man.* London: Methuen, 1987

Walzer, M. *Spheres of Justice.* Oxford: Martin Robertson, 1983

Williams, B. 'The Idea of Equality, in P. Laslett and W. G. Runciman (eds.), *Philosophy, Politics and Society,* second series. Oxford: Blackwell, 1964

the review of
metaphysics

a philosophical quarterly

ISSN 0034-6632

JUNE 1990 | **VOL. XLIII, No. 4** | **ISSUE No. 172** | **$9.00**

articles

critical exchange

books received

philosophical abstracts

announcements

index

philosophical abstracts   *announcements*   *index*

Individual Subscriptions $23.00   Institutional Subscriptions $35.00   Student/Retired Subscriptions $12.00

Jude P. Dougherty, Editor

The Catholic University of America, Washington, D.C. 20064

INQUIRY

An Interdisciplinary Journal of Philosophy

EDITOR: ALASTAIR HANNAY

Selected Articles from Vol. 33, 1990:

Carl Paul Ellerman: New Notes from Underground (with rejoinder by *Stephen R.L. Clark:* Notes on the Underground) (No.1)

Will Kymlicka: Two Theories of Justice (Brian Barry, *Theories of Justice*, vol. 1 of *A Treatise on Social Justice*) (No.1)

Ernest LePore: Subjectivity and Environmentalism (No.2)

Andrew Mason: On Explaining Political Disagreement: The Notion of an Essentially Contested Concept (No.1)

Alfred Nordmann: Goodbye and Farewell: Siegel vs. Feyerabend (No.3)

Michael Pendlebury: Sense Experiences and Their Contents: A Defence of the Propositional Account (No.2)

Herman Philipse: The Absolute Network Theory of Language: On the Philosophical Foundations of Paul Churchland's Scientific Realism (with reply by *Paul M. Churchland*) (No.2)

Joseph Rouse: The Narrative Reconstruction of Science (No.3) .

Arnold Zuboff: One Self: The Logic of Experience (No.1)

INQUIRY is published quarterly by

UNIVERSITETSFORLAGET

Subscription to be ordered from: Universitetsforlaget (Norwegian University Press), P.O. Box 2959 Tøyen, 0608 Oslo 6, Norway, or U.S. Office: Publications Expediting Inc., 200 Meacham Ave., Elmont, NY 11003, USA.

✂